FISHING RIGS

FOR
FRESH &
SALT
WATER

FISHING RIGS

FOR FRESH & SALT WATER

VLAD EVANOFF

Illustrated by
the author

HARPER & ROW
PUBLISHERS
New York   Hagerstown
San Francisco   London

FIRST EDITION

Library of Congress Cataloging in Publication Data

Evanoff, Vlad.
  Fishing rigs for fresh and salt water.
  Includes index.
  1. Fishing rigs. I. Title.
SH452.9.R5E93   799.1′2′028   76–26221
ISBN 0–06–011257–3

77 78 79 80 81 10 9 8 7 6 5 4 3 2 1

CONTENTS

ACKNOWLEDGMENTS

The author wishes to express his appreciation to the many fresh- and saltwater anglers who have sent information and sketches of their favorite rigs from such publications as *Long Island Fisherman*, *Salt Water Sportsman* and the *Garcia Fishing Annual*, as well as to the many outdoors writers who have had various rigs described in print.

I would especially like to thank the E. I. du Pont de Nemours & Co. Inc. Plastics Department and Stren Fishing Products for permission to use some of their knot drawings and knot-tying information in this book.

I would also like to thank O. Mustad & Son, Inc., and the Wright & McGill Company for permission to use some of their hook illustrations and information.

PREFACE

One of the main reasons some anglers catch more fish than others is that they know how to tie the proper rig or leader for the fishing they plan to do. Veteran fishermen are very fussy about their rigs and prefer to tie their own. A beginner who doesn't know how to tie rigs will catch fewer and smaller fish and lose many of them.

Many things can cause a fishing rig to be improperly tied. It can be tied of leader material that is too thin or too thick. It can be tied too high on the fishing line or too low. It can have the wrong hook pattern or the wrong hook size. The sinker or weight may be too light or too heavy. Or the sinker or weight may be the wrong kind for the fishing being done.

While you can buy some good rigs in a fishing-tackle store, they are expensive. By buying the leader material, hardware, hooks and sinkers or weights separately and tying your own rigs you can cut the price at least in half.

Rigs are constantly being lost or broken off, so the money you save by tying your own can add up. Some of the best fishing spots in fresh and salt water are found around such obstructions as sunken wrecks, bridge and pier pilings, rocks, coral, submerged trees and logs, weeds, barnacles, mussels and similar hazards that can cause rigs to get snagged or fouled. Big fish with sharp teeth often bite off rigs and leaders or lines, so you should always have spares on hand.

Thus there is another reason anglers who tie their own rigs catch more fish. If they had bought ready-made rigs they might well avoid fishing in hazardous spots. Having made their own, they tend to feel that if they lose a rig, so what; it didn't cost too much and they can always make up a new one. So they fish the worst spots for rigs—which are the best spots to catch fish.

Tying your own rigs enables you to suit your personal tastes and preferences, the area being fished, the fish being sought and the bait or lure being used. Also, you can fashion the rigs to meet changing conditions and situations that arise on the fishing grounds, to satisfy a particular need or to solve a certain fishing problem.

Until now there has been no book devoted entirely to the most popular fresh- and saltwater fishing rigs, showing how to tie them and how to use them effectively. It is hoped that this book will fill such a need and that anglers who learn how to tie these rigs and use them properly will catch more and bigger fish.

1. SNAPS, SWIVELS AND OTHER HARDWARE

There are many kinds of snaps, swivels, snap swivels, spreaders and other hardware that can be utilized in making up rigs for both fresh- and saltwater fishing. They are used as connectors or for quick changing of lures or for keeping the hooks and snells and leaders from tangling. And in the casting or trolling and retrieving of certain lures, swivels also help to prevent the line from twisting.

When you purchase such terminal hardware for fishing, choose smaller, lighter and finer snaps, swivels and connectors for fresh-water fishing than for saltwater. Use the smaller and lighter ones with light tackle or for wary fish; the heavier and stronger ones for big fish, especially in salt water. Many anglers make the mistake of using swivels, snaps and other hardware that are too big and too strong for the fish they are seeking and the tackle they are using. Since most of this hardware is extremely strong for its size, it is much better to use the smaller sizes. And do not use more hardware than is absolutely necessary. Usually one or two small- or medium-size snaps or swivels will serve the purpose.

Most swivels, snaps and other hardware are made of brass, steel or stainless steel. Some are also silver-plated, chromed or painted. The shiny silver or chromed snaps and swivels can be used for most

1

fish and fishing; but when you are after bluefish, cero, Spanish or king mackerel you should choose dull brown or black hardware, since these fish have been known to hit shiny swivels and bite through the line or leader.

TWO TYPES OF BARREL SWIVELS

The barrel swivel has many uses in making up rigs for casting, trolling or bottom fishing. It has two eyelets—one on each end that revolves freely inside a "barrel." Two types are in common use today. The first has wire eyes that are twisted on each end and a single wire inside the barrel. In the second, more modern swivel, the eye is formed by doubling the wire and both ends are inserted into the barrel. Most barrel swivels range in graduating sizes from No. 12, which is the smallest, up to 5/0 or more. They test from about 30 pounds up to several hundred pounds.

But ordinary barrel swivels do not always revolve freely, especially under a load or in trolling with lures that spin. Therefore many angers prefer the ball-bearing type of swivel, such as the Sampo. This has a machined two-part body and steel ball bearings inside. There is a split ring on each end for the freshwater series and a stronger, welded ring for the saltwater series. The smaller sizes test 10 or 12 pounds, while the heavy-duty swivels test up to 600 pounds.

SAMPO BALL-BEARING SWIVELS

Another swivel made for heavy saltwater fishing is the Tunalin, which tests up to 900 pounds. It is made of solid brass in two parts, with the ends flattened and holes for the attachment of the line or leader.

The bead chain swivel consists of a series of small, round stainless-steel beads. Each bead acts as a swivel and doesn't rust, bind or jam, which helps prevent the line's twisting. Bead chain swivels usually come with a ring or eye on each end to which the line or leader can be tied. Or they may have snaps on one or both ends. You can obtain them in various sizes, lengths and strengths.

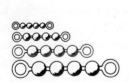
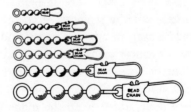

BEAD CHAIN SWIVELS
AND SNAP SWIVELS

Snaps of different types are available for making rigs for casting, trolling or bottom fishing. They are usually used on the end of a fishing line or leader so that you can easily change hooks, lures, baits, sinkers or rigs. The most common type of snap is the safety-pin style, which has a sharp bend in the wire loop that opens and closes like an ordinary safety pin. This is a fairly good snap for freshwater and light saltwater use, but it tends to open under a severe strain, pull or weight.

The interlock snap opens and closes like a safety pin, too, but the end of the wire loop or eye has a curve or bend that locks more securely than the snap mentioned above. Its round eye or loop permits a lure to work more freely and have better action than the sharp-bend snap. The interlock snap is good for freshwater and light saltwater fishing.

The third type of snap is the all-wire lock-around design, whose long loop or eye is semiround. Most popular is the Pompanette, made of stainless steel and very reliable and strong. It comes in strengths from 18 to 300 pounds and can be used for every kind of saltwater fish up to marlin, tuna and sharks.

Good snaps are made from stiff spring wire and open and close only under considerable tension. Even so, snaps will sometimes open during fishing or during a fight with a fish. They also weaken after they have landed several fish or a big fish or after they have been opened and closed many times. Always examine a snap in the course of fishing to make sure it hasn't opened. And if you have any doubts about the strength of the old snap, change to a new one.

Add a snap to a barrel swivel and you have a snap swivel, which is the way most snaps are used. They are great time-savers in casting, trolling or bottom fishing, enabling the angler to change baits, lures, hooks, leaders and sinkers quickly. Although many anglers like to tie their lure directly to the monofilament leader when fishing for wary fish, this can be a nuisance if you are using different lures and changing them frequently. So most anglers who are trolling tie one snap swivel on the end of their line and attach another to

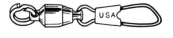

SAMPO BALL-BEARING SNAP SWIVELS

the end of the leader. But make sure that the eye on your snap swivel is big and wide and round enough to bring out the best action in your lure. If you are just casting or if your leader is attached directly to the lure, then all you need is a single snap swivel on the end of your line to change lures or baits.

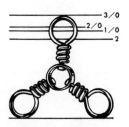

3-WAY SWIVEL

One of the most commonly used pieces of hardware for a light trolling rig or a bottom-fishing rig is the three-way swivel, which has three eyes that turn inside an open ring. When making up a bottom rig, tie the fishing line to one eye, the hook and leader to

CONNECTING   LINKS

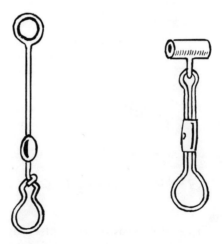

TWO TYPES OF FISH FINDERS

another eye and attach the sinker to the third eye. These three-way swivels come in three or four sizes and strengths for light and heavy bottom fishing. The larger sizes are also used to make up surf-fishing rigs.

Somewhat similar to the three-way swivel is the cross-line swivel, with three eyes set at right angles to a barrel. A variation has two eyes on the barrel and a lockfast snap set at right angles. Here you can quickly add or remove a hook with snell or leader. Both types of swivels can be used for making up bottom rigs.

Then we have the connecting links with wire eyes or snaps on both ends for rapid attachment of snells, leaders, lines, lures and hooks. The most common type is the connecting link with wire loops on both ends and a sliding metal sleeve in the middle. Here you depress the wire at one end of the metal sleeve to slide it toward the wire loop, close it by sliding it back toward the center. These connecting links also come with a small eye or loop on one end and a larger loop or eye on the other.

The double snap swivel, with a lockfast snap or a safety snap on each end of a barrel swivel, is another method of connection. This type is also made with bead chain swivels and snaps on both ends. It can be very handy, in trolling, for quick changing of leaders, lures, hooks, rigs and weights.

For making surf-fishing rigs or bottom-fishing rigs where you don't want the fish to feel the weight of the sinker when it mouths and runs with the bait, the "fish-finder" devices are often used. Of the two basic types, one is the old-time, all-metal fish-finder with a big ring on one end of a wire bar and a barrel swivel and lockfast snap on the other end. The more modern type has a nylon sleeve with a hole and a connecting link attached to it. They both work on the same principle. The fish line is run through the hole or sleeve and a barrel swivel is tied to the end of the line. Then the hook and leader is tied to this barrel swivel. The sinker, usually a pyramid type, is attached to the snap or connecting link. After being cast out from a beach, the sinker goes down to the bottom and digs into the sand. A fish that grabs the baited hook can run and pull the line through the hole or sleeve and not feel the weight of the sinker.

Some rigs call for the use of split rings, especially in conjunction with spinners, spoons or other lures aimed at bringing out the best action. Instead of tying the leader or line directly to the small eye of the lure, you add the split ring to the front of the lure and tie your leader or line to that. You can also use split rings to hold single or treble hooks to the tail of the lure, especially when you plan to change the hooks every so often. Of course, many lures come with split rings, and there is no need to add more.

Split rings can also be used as "stops" when you want to prevent a float or sinker from sliding down the leader or line. Split rings come in different sizes and strengths. The smaller rings are used for freshwater and light saltwater fishing, the larger ones for heavy saltwater fishing.

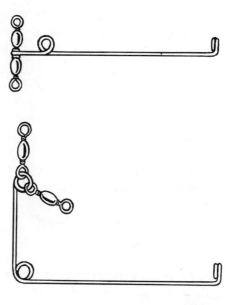

SPREADERS FOR BOTTOM FISHING RIGS

FLOUNDER SPREADER

Finally, we have the various hook holders, connectors, arms and spreaders, which keep the hooks and snells away from the main fishing line in bottom fishing. Some are also used for trolling more than one lure at a time.

One of the simplest hook connectors you can add to your bottom rig is a short length of rubber or plastic tubing. Slip this over the three-way swivel where it is attached to the line and snell. Other hook holders have free-swinging arms between two barrel swivels that keep the hook and snell away from the main fishing line. Still others that serve the same purpose have rigid arms in the shape of a T or L.

Special spreaders for flounder fishing are made of rigid or flexible wire and have a swivel in the center to which the fishing line is attached. Below that is a snap to hold the sinker, and an arm runs from the center on each side, to which the snelled hooks are attached. These can be bought in most coastal fishing-tackle shops.

Some of the largest and strongest spreaders are used for trolling in both fresh and salt water. Either L-shaped or formed into triangles of various sizes, they are usually made from heavy wire and have three eyes. The main fishing line is attached to one eye; the leader with hook or lure is attached to another eye; and the sinker or weight is tied to the remaining eye.

There are also spreaders made from heavy wire that are used to troll multiple lures of different types or weights at the same time. Most of them have two arms, but in recent years anglers have also been using the so-called umbrella rigs, which have several arms and are used to troll up to a dozen tube teasers and lures.

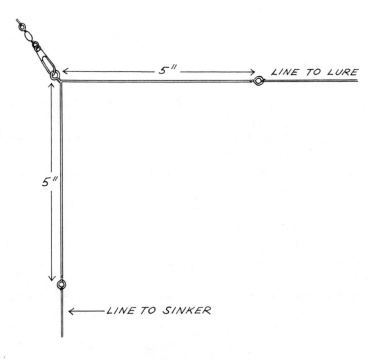

SPREADER FOR TROLLING

2. FLOATS AND BOBBERS

Some of the rigs in this book call for a float or bobber. Though floats and bobbers are more common in freshwater fishing, they have their uses in saltwater fishing. Their main functions are to suspend a bait at a certain level and indicate when a fish takes the bait. But they can also be used to provide casting weight for light lures or baits, as well as to drift a bait out in the current, or with the tide or wind. Some floats act as splashers to attract fish to the scene. Floats can additionally serve on surf-fishing or bottom rigs to keep the bait off the bottom so that crabs and undesirable fish can't reach it.

Floats and bobbers are made in a wide variety of sizes, shapes and materials. Many fishermen going after suspicious fish use a float or bobber that is too large and heavy. For best results the float or bobber should be just big enough to suspend the bait at a certain level or keep it from the bottom or weeds. And the float or bobber should be pulled under the water easily, with little or no resistance. This is especially true in clear, shallow fresh water where the fish not only feel the pull of the line and float but can also see it bobbing on the surface.

 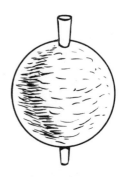

CORK FLOATS

Almost everyone who has fished for panfish in fresh water with a cane pole knows how to make the simplest float of all. This is an ordinary bottle stopper in which you puncture a hole through the center, run the fishing line or leader through and then force a stick into the hole to keep the float in place on the line.

You can buy cork floats in many sizes and shapes for freshwater fishing. Most of them come in round, oval or oblong shapes and are either plain or painted in different colors. Still other floats and bobbers are made from balsa wood. These cork and balsa floats may have holes running through the center for slipping on the line, or clips, coils of wire or other devices for holding on line or leader.

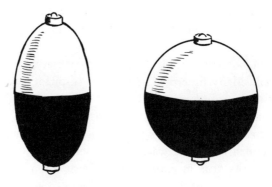

PLASTIC FLOATS

In recent years floats and bobbers made from plastic have taken over the market and are used by most freshwater anglers. One of the most popular is the ball type, but others may be pear-shaped, oval or oblong. They are usually red and white and have clips or wire hooks or similar devices for attaching to the line. Some have a spring action that holds the line or leader firmly and prevents the float from sliding up and down.

One of the most sensitive floats or bobbers you can use is several inches long and rarely more than a half inch thick. Many are made today from plastic or balsa wood, but the natural porcupine quill is still hard to beat for wary fish. The porcupine quill usually has a wire eyelet at the lower end and a rubber band around the middle. The line goes under the rubber band and is attached to the eyelet.

Though some porcupine quills have lighter-colored upper ends, most are black or dark brown and somewhat difficult to see in the water. You can easily paint or spray two or three inches of the quill with white or yellow paint for greater visibility.

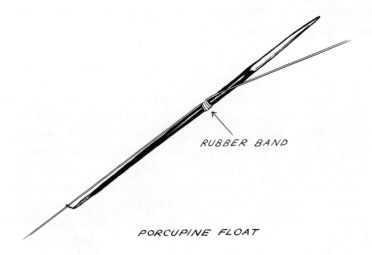

RUBBER BAND

PORCUPINE FLOAT

Some of the floats used in fresh water are heavy, and you can cast these with a light bait a good distance with a spinning or even a bait-casting outfit. When using a heavy bait, such as a big minnow, frog or crayfish, you have enough weight to cast even if the float is a light one. But with small worms, nymphs, grasshoppers, crickets or similar light baits you need a heavier float or some weight on the line.

Casting a bait with a float or bobber that is too high up on the line can be difficult if not impossible. You can solve this by tying a sliding knot around your line or leader, then sliding a shirt button up on the line. Next get an ordinary bottle cork or round cork and bore a hole wide enough to take a narrow plastic tube or crow quill. Push this into the hole and then slip the cork on your line or leader. Add a split-shot sinker or two a few inches above the hook.

To use this rig you adjust the knot on your line or leader at the depth you want to fish. Then when you are ready to cast, the float will slide down to the split-shot sinkers and you can cast it easily. After the float lands on the water, feed some slack line. The hook and bait will sink, while the float will rise and stop at the knot. When you hook a fish or want to check your bait, the float will slide down to the split-shot sinker again.

The more modern, clear plastic floats, or "bubble" floats, are favored by many anglers using spinning tackle. These are hollow and can be filled with water or mineral oil to provide casting weight. They are small and compact and cast far, and being almost invisible in the water, they don't frighten fish. For this reason they are especially popular for trout fishing in streams, rivers and lakes. But they can also be used for other fish, such as bass and panfish.

The plastic bubble floats are usually round or oval in shape. Some have removable plugs or stoppers, others spring-loaded plungers that can be pushed into the central globe when they are being filled with liquid. Though of course water is available right at the fishing spot, many anglers prefer to fill their plastic floats at home with mineral oil, since the oil doesn't evaporate.

There are many ways that the plastic bubble floats can be employed. You may tie it on the end of your line, then add a three-foot leader and tie on the fly or lure. This is a good way to use either wet or dry flies, nymphs, streamers and bass or panfish bugs; small plastic worms, spinners, spoons and jigs can be substituted.

The bubble can also be tied on the end of your line or leader and the flies attached on short droppers in front of it. You can use one, two or even three flies spaced about a foot and a half apart. Or you can try different natural baits, such as worms, crickets, grasshoppers and minnows. Here you would tie the bubble on the end of the line and add a leader with hook about three or four feet behind it— about the longest length you can cast with ease.

In most of the above methods the plastic bubble is filled so that it has weight for casting but still floats on top of the water. But you can also fill the bubble completely with water so that it sinks slowly and you can then retrieve your flies, lures or baits gradually at various depths.

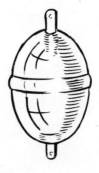

PLASTIC BUBBLE FLOATS

Many of the floats already mentioned are also used for saltwater fishing. But because the baits are often larger and the stronger currents and tides require heavier weights on the line, floats are usually bigger for saltwater than for freshwater fishing.

Cork floats of various types, usually round or oval-shaped, are still utilized to a great extent in saltwater fishing. For big baits anglers often use the larger cork floats found on commercial fishing nets. In recent years, however, more and more such floats have been made from plastic or Styrofoam in various sizes, shapes and designs. They usually come painted in light, visible colors such as white, yellow, orange, pink or red. The bright fluorescent versions are popular because of their high visibility.

Many saltwater anglers make their own floats by cutting Styrofoam into desired sizes, usually square or rectangular in shape. Then they make a slot on both sides of the Styrofoam and wrap their leader or line around it with a half hitch. When a fish is hooked, the foam breaks free.

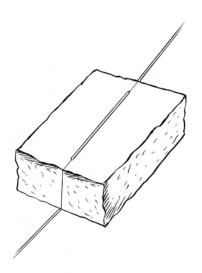

STYROFOAM FLOAT

Another float used by saltwater anglers, especially with big baits, is an ordinary rubber balloon, which is inflated to the size desired and then knotted to keep the air in. Tie a snap swivel to the balloon, attach your fishing line to one of the eyes of the barrel swivel, then add a hook with leader to the snap. Such floats are usually used by shore, pier and jetty anglers who want to send a bait out into deeper water. Fishing at the mouth of an inlet with an outgoing tide or from a pier or shore when the wind is blowing away from land is most effective.

Other good floats can be made from the various plastic containers found on supermarkets shelves. For instance, tie your line or leader around the neck or under the cap of a plastic lemon-juice container. Larger floats can be made from the big white jugs holding cleaners and bleaches. Some of these even have handles to which you can attach your line or leader with weaker line that will break off when a fish hits or is hooked.

Surf anglers often use floats on their bottom rigs to keep the bait suspended above the bottom so that crabs and other pests do not steal it. Two types of floats are usually used: the common round cork float mentioned earlier, and the long, narrow type, which often comes in fluorescent colors. These are attached on the leader between the main fishing line and the hook. The closer you connect the float to the hook, the higher the bait will be off the bottom.

Anglers fishing for sea trout in southern waters often prefer a popping cork or float with a hollow or grooved head. The shrimp bait usually used with this float is suspended about two feet below it. The float is cast out and then popped so that it makes a splash, which attracts sea trout to the scene.

POPPING FLOAT

Somewhat similar are the wooden blocks or dowels favored by anglers fishing for striped bass and pollock in New England waters. Behind a wooden dowel about four or five inches long they add a leader about two feet long, then attach a tiny spoon, jig or feathered hook to the end of the leader. The wooden block provides casting weight even with a surf rod. And the block can be "chugged" or "popped" on top of the water to attract the fish. Much the same thing can be accomplished with surface popping or swimming plugs instead of the block. Only here you can remove the tail hook before attaching the trailer with the other lure.

3. SINKERS AND WEIGHTS

The lowly sinker is taken for granted by most fresh- and saltwater anglers, yet it plays a big part in fishing. Choosing the right type of sinker of the proper weight for the rig you are using and the fishing being done can influence your fishing success. You have to take into consideration the depth of the water, the strength of the tide or current, the type of bottom and your tackle and line before you can select the proper sinker.

The most important function of a sinker in bottom fishing is to take your rig down to the bottom and hold it there so that the fish can see and take the bait. Sinkers that are too light or of improper design may not hold, and the tide and current may lift the rig too high off the bottom for the fish to see it. On the other hand, a sinker that is too heavy stays put in one spot and doesn't give the bait any movement or action. A sinker of ideal weight holds bottom when the line is still but can be lifted off the bottom and carried a short distance in the current or tide to give the bait some life and carry it into new territory.

So the experienced bottom fisherman carries sinkers in several weights and changes them as conditions require. If the tide is running strong, he adds a heavier sinker. If it weakens, he changes to a lighter weight. If the angler is using light tackle, he uses light sinkers. If he is using heavy tackle or thick lines or is fishing in deep water, he uses heavier sinkers.

Sinkers are usually made from lead. Today the angler has a wide variety of types and designs to choose from to suit almost every kind of fresh- or saltwater fishing. Sinkers can be bought in most fishing-tackle stores, or you can get a mold and easily pour your own.

One of the lightest and smallest sinkers is the round split-shot or BB sinker, which comes in four or five sizes. It has a split about halfway through, and the line or leader is pinched between the split-shot with pliers. Anywhere from one to a half dozen are used on the leader or line to get the bait down in a current. These are very popular for fishing in streams for trout, bass or panfish. You can also use the split-shot sinkers on a leader or line when still-fishing to get the bait down deeper and hold it there. Or you can add them between bait and float to keep the bait below the surface. Some anglers put them on short droppers hanging from the leader or line.

SPLIT SHOT

CLINCHER

RUBBERCORE

THREE KINDS OF LIGHT SINKERS

But split-shot sinkers tend to damage a thin line or leader and are difficult to remove, so many anglers prefer the wraparound strip leads with bait, flies or lures in a stream or river. These narrow, thin, soft lead strips are about one and a half inches long and are available in paper-match-type packages. They can be torn out readily and wrapped around the leader and line to provide sinking weight. Wrap the strip on your leader or line by starting at the middle of the lead strip and working toward each end. Make sure that the ends are pinched down neatly so that they don't pick up debris or get hung up on the bottom.

You can also buy round soft lead wire. It comes in different diameters and is wrapped around a line or leader like the strip lead. This wire comes coiled in a handy plastic disk package like nylon leader material.

Another light sinker used often on a line or leader to get a bait or lure deeper is the clincher sinker. Also called the "clamp-on" or "pinch-on" sinker, this is an elongated weight with ears or folding lugs on each end that are bent around the line or leader to hold it in place. The line or leader runs through a deep slit in the body of the sinker, and the entire sinker can be squeezed with pliers to hold it firmly in place. Clincher sinkers can be used in fresh water with fly rods, cane poles or spinning tackle to take baits down to certain depths. The larger sizes can hold a bait or lure below the surface in slow trolling. And they serve in salt water to take a bait out in a current or tide and keep it below the surface.

But clincher sinkers can damage a line or leader, so the Water Gremlin Company came up with the Rubbercore sinker, similar to the clincher sinker but with a rubber-lined slit and a rubber tip on each end. The line and leader are thus protected from wearing, rubbing or chafing. The Rubbercore is also easy to attach and remove.

In freshwater fishing the most widely used sinker for bottom-fishing rigs and some trolling rigs is the "dipsey" or bass-casting sinker, a pear-shaped weight with a wire eye on the narrow end. This wire usually swivels or turns inside the sinker. Though they

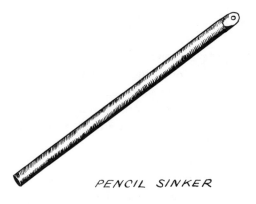

PENCIL SINKER

tend to roll on a hard, smooth bottom, especially in a current, the dipsey sinkers hold fairly well on rocky or gravel bottoms. You can obtain them in weights from one-eighth ounce up to eight or ten ounces.

Another sinker used in fresh water, especially by steelhead or trout anglers fishing streams and rivers, is the "pencil" sinker, which as its name implies, is long, narrow and round in shape. It comes in various lengths, diameters and weights and tends to bounce along a rocky bottom without getting snagged. It can also be used for trolling over such bottoms.

A good sinker for bottom fishing in both fresh and salt water is the egg or oval sinker. This has a hole running through the center and is slipped on a fishing line or leader above a barrel swivel, which acts as a stop. A leader and hook is tied to the other end of the barrel swivel. The egg sinker works like most "fish-finder" rigs: a fish can pull line through the sinker or a ring without feeling the weight. This rig can be used in bottom fishing or in fishing from a drifting boat; in trolling, it can take a bait or lure deeper. Because of its rounded shape it doesn't tend to foul or snag on the bottom as often as other sinkers. Egg sinkers usually weigh from about one-eighth ounce up to six or eight ounces.

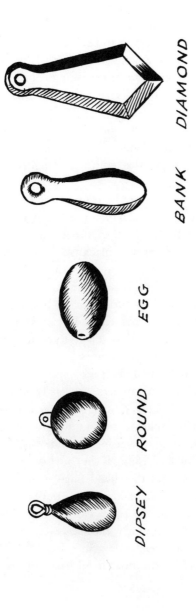

DIAMOND

BANK

EGG

ROUND

DIPSEY

SINKERS USED IN BOTTOM FISHING

The basic sinker used for bottom fishing in salt water is the "bank" sinker. Fairly long, with several sides, and the eye cast into the head section, it is a good all-round sinker for all types of bottom, and it slides over rocks without snagging too readily. It comes in weights from one-half ounce up to a pound or more. Bank sinkers in the lighter weights are used in freshwater fishing. Some anglers favor a special type that is bent or curved like a slip sinker, and use it as they use the egg sinker.

In deep water where you need a lot of lead to get down and hold bottom in strong tides, the "diamond" sinker is valuable. This is a flat sinker with beveled edges that comes in weights up to a pound and more.

If you fish over rocky bottoms, the round-type sinker, shaped like a ball and with an eye on top to which the line is tied, is less likely to snag or hang up in the rocks than others. It is popular among anglers who fish in the Atlantic for blackfish or tautog.

The pyramid sinker has long been a favorite with surf fishermen fishing on the bottom with bait. It has four flat, triangular sides and sharp edges or corners that dig into the sand bottom and help the sinker to hold despite waves and tides. It can also be used over other soft bottoms, such as mud or clay. Pyramid sinkers usually come in weights from one to eight ounces, with those of three, four, five and six ounces used most of the time.

Another sinker used by surf anglers, especially in Pacific waters, is the "bulldozer," shaped like a Y, with the ring for the line in the center of the fork. This sinker comes in weights from one to six ounces and has good holding power in the sand.

Still another sinker for surf fishing is the "surf weight" type, which has thick but soft wire tines that bend fairly easily. The tines are embedded in a cone-shaped lead and are bent outward at a 45-degree angle before casting. When the rig is cast out and the sinker falls to the bottom, the wire tines bury themselves in the sand and can hold the bait in place without rolling in a heavy surf. When you pull on the line to reel in, the tines bend back and free the sinker from the sand.

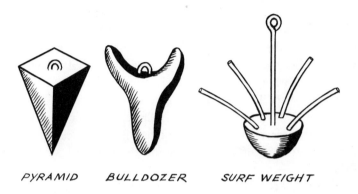

PYRAMID   BULLDOZER   SURF WEIGHT

SINKERS USED IN SURF FISHING

There are many other kinds of specialized sinkers with peculiar shapes or designs intended for specific types of fishing—flat, oval, bell-shaped, cylindrical and a few odd shapes. Some of these are sold all over the country, while others are found only in local tackle shops. Amost all tackle stores carry some of the basic sinkers. Anglers who do a lot of fishing often buy a mold and pour their own sinkers, especially if they can get scrap lead at a reasonable price.

Trolling and casting weights are used to keep baits or lures down deep and are available in a variety of styles. Some also serve to prevent the line from twisting, as do keels or rudders, for example, whose weight is suspended below the line or leader. One of the simplest of these is the Keelart sinker, which is shaped like a heart when flat. Bent around a line, it forms a light keel for light-tackle use. It comes in weights from one-eighth to one ounce.

Among the most popular trolling weights and keels are the thicker, heavier types that have eyes on both ends for attaching the line and leader. The preferred cigar-shaped and crescent-shaped leads are available, in weights up to a pound or so, with the two- to eight-ounce sizes used most often. The keel-shaped leads usually range from one-sixteenth to four ounces, for most fresh and light saltwater fishing, but there are heavier ones for special situations.

Actually the slim, cigar-shaped trolling weight can be used for most fresh- and saltwater fishing, since it is made with bead chain swivels by several companies. Usually it has several beads in front of the lead with an eye on one end; the other end has more beads, ending in a snap. The fishing line is attached in front of the trolling weight—which functions also to help prevent line twist—and a leader anywhere from two feet up to thirty feet can be attached to the snap. Then, of course, you add the lure or bait on the end of the leader.

These weights can be used in fast trolling to keep a lure just below the surface, as is common in fishing for school tuna, albacore or bonito. At slower speeds the trolling weight will carry your lure or bait deeper, depending on how much line you let out. To get down still deeper you troll even more slowly with heavier weights, or you can use a wire line on your reel. With such a weight you can tell if you are near the bottom or near rocks by letting out a few feet of line every so often, and by bouncing bottom with the trolling weight you can make sure you are deep enough.

Such trolling weights can also be used when you are drifting in a boat and want to get a bait or lure down deep. By letting line out as the boat drifts, you can have your bait or lure traveling at different depths until you get a strike or a fish. Then you can mark your line and drift at that depth as long as the action lasts.

Trolling weights in the lighter sizes can also be used as casting weights to get light lures out a good distance. Here the weight is added on the line or leader anywhere from a few inches to about three feet ahead of the lure. Anything longer is difficult to cast.

A specialized trolling weight is the "cannonball" sinker, a round iron sinker weighing up to a pound or two, used along the Pacific coast in slow trolling for salmon in deep water. It is attached to a sinker-release device on the line, which frees the heavy sinker when

BEAD-CHAIN TROLLING WEIGHTS

CANNONBALL SINKER WITH
QUICK RELEASE DEVICE

a salmon strikes so the angler can fight the fish without the additional weight.

Other anglers use various types of "underwater outriggers" that have heavy weights attached to a strong line. The fishing line is connected to this by means of a clip, and the two lines are lowered together into the depths. When a fish strikes, the clip releases the fishing line from the weight.

Finally, we have the various kinds of planers, which are employed in trolling to take a bait or lure way down without putting too much strain on the rod and line. When trolled slowly, the planer digs deep into the water and moves smoothly at a depth that can often be set in advance. Most of the planers have a tripping device that, when activated by a strike or a hooked fish, makes it turn and prevents it from diving, so it offers less resistance.

So, as we can see, sinkers and weights have many uses in fresh- and saltwater fishing and in making up casting, drifting or trolling rigs. It pays to have an assortment of them at home and on a fishing trip so that you will be prepared for different fishing methods and situations.

TROLLING PLANER

4. HOOKS

All the parts of your rigs or terminal tackle are vital, but the hook on the end of your snell or leader is the most important single item. After all, the main purpose of the other tackle—the rod, reel, line and rig—is to get the hook or hooks to the spot where the fish can see and grab it. Only the hook makes actual contact with the fish. You can have the best fishing tackle in the world, but if the hook is weak or of the wrong size or pattern you may fail to hook your fish or lose it after you do hook it.

Most veteran anglers know this because they had to learn the hard way, through trial and error, that fishing success often depends on the right choice of hook. These anglers give close attention to the selection of the right style or pattern, size and temper of the hooks they plan to utilize. It pays to study the various designs, parts, uses and qualities of the hooks you choose when tying up rigs for casting, trolling or bottom fishing.

Basically, the design of the fishhook hasn't changed much through the centuries. Curved hooks with barbs, very similar to the ones employed today, were in use 3,000 years ago. However, there have been great improvements in the variety of patterns, the quality of the steel, the temper and finishes of modern hooks. The earlier hooks were made mostly by hand and were less uniform and often un-dependable. Today, fishhook manufacturers have machines that automatically clean the wire, straighten it and cut it to length; cut the barb, then slice, mill and grind the point; forge and bend the hook and form the eye. Such machines can be adjusted so that any size hook can be made. The resulting fishhook, if made by a reputable company, is a precision product, uniform and reliable. Among the leading fishhook manufacturers are O. Mustad & Son of Norway, Edgar Sealey, Ltd., of England and the Wright & McGill Company of Denver, Colorado.

To understand hooks you should know something about their various parts and construction. Hooks vary a great deal in size, shape, design, thickness of wire, length of shank, bends, eyes and finishes. Take the shank, for example—the part running from the eye of the hook up to the bend. The same pattern of hook can be made with a short, regular or long shank. Regular-length shanks are applicable for most fish and fishing, but there are times, in fishing for certain fish and using certain baits, when other lengths are better.

A short shank is often used when you want to hide the hook inside a bait and make it less visible to a wary fish. It is also good for small baits such as salmon eggs and when fishing with live sardines or anchovies in the Pacific for the hook-and-leader-shy albacore and

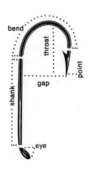

PARTS OF A HOOK

yellowtail. Short-shank hooks are also used to tie flies such as spiders and variants.

A hook with a long shank is suitable for fish with sharp teeth that would cut through a line or leader, and for fish that tend to swallow a bait. And it holds certain baits better or more than one bait on a single hook. Long-shanked hooks are best for tying flies such as streamers and bucktails.

Hook shanks are usually made straight, with an even thickness or diameter, but some have tapered shanks and eyes to help reduce their weight, especially in tying dry flies. Some shanks may have a curve or a hump, and still others may have slices or small barbs that hold natural baits, such as worms, better along the entire length of the hook.

Hooks also come with different points. The spear point found on many hooks runs in a straight line from point to barb. This point requires quite a bit of force to penetrate and may not go beyond the barb if it isn't set with force or if it strikes the hard part of a fish's mouth.

Much better is the "hollow" point, which is rounded out or dished out from the tip to the point of the barb. This makes the point thinner and shallower, but it is a good penetrating point and holds well in fish with soft mouths. In the case of fish with tough, hard mouths, it may spring or bend and not penetrate too well.

The needle-point hook is round like a needle and tapers from the tip of the point to the barb. It penetrates quickly and deeply in fish with soft mouths. If it is properly made and tempered right, it can be strong. But if not well made, it will tend to bend or break, especially at the fine point.

The rolled-in point is bent in toward the shank and resembles a claw, talon or beak. In fact, these hooks are often called "claw" or "beak" hooks in the trade. The point is curved inward in line with the eye and provides a direct line of pull. This point may take a shallower bite than others, but once it is set beyond the barb it holds well and is difficult to disgorge or throw.

Then there is the knife-edge point, which has two flat sides along its single inner edge, just like a knife; and the diamond or triangulated point, which has three cutting edges. These hooks are used for fish with hard mouths, such as tarpon, or in big-game fishing, since they penetrate easier, faster and deeper.

Hooks also come with different types of eyes, such as the ball or ringed, tapered, looped or needle. The ball or ringed eye is the most common. Here the wire, of uniform diameter throughout, is bent into a circle. This is a good, strong eye that can be used for bait fishing or behind a spinner or for trolling.

In a hook with a tapered eye, the end of the wire forming the ring decreases in diameter, this part being thinner than the rest of the hook. Such hooks are often used in tying dry flies to reduce the weight of the hook so that the fly floats better and higher. It is also used on some of the larger hooks for bait fishing and for lures and even for saltwater hooks where a smaller eye is desired. But such tapering tends to weaken the eye of the hook, and it may open or break under a heavy strain.

The looped eye is more or less oval-shaped and runs back along the hook shank, where the end may be tapered. In this eye there is no sharp edge or end at the eye itself to cut the line or leader.

The needle eye, resembling the eye of a sewing needle, doesn't bulge out at the end like the other eyes. It is popular in big-game fishing because it is strong and small enough to be buried inside a bait that is rigged for trolling.

There are also eyeless hooks with tapered ends or knobbed, marked or flatted shanks, used for snelled hooks. Eyes on hooks can be turned away from the point to provide more gap space. Such "turned up" eyes are usually found on small, short-shanked hooks. The eye may also be "turned down" toward the point, for tying flies and for tying on leaders and snells for bait fishing.

The bend, or curved part, of a hook may also vary. Though most hooks have a round or nearly round bend, others may be bent at an angle, or they may be offset or kirbed, the point facing either to the left or right when you hold the hook so that the shank runs in a straight line away from you.

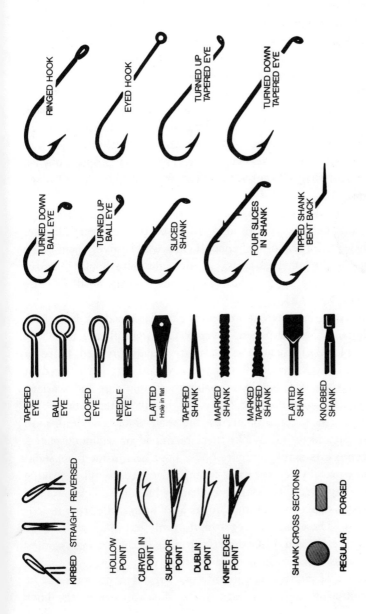

RINGED HOOK

EYED HOOK

TURNED UP
TAPERED EYE

TURNED DOWN
TAPERED EYE

TURNED DOWN
BALL EYE

TURNED UP
BALL EYE

SLICED
SHANK

FOUR SLICES
IN SHANK

TIPPED SHANK
BENT BACK

TAPERED
EYE

BALL
EYE

LOOPED
EYE

NEEDLE
EYE

FLATTED
Hole in flat

TAPERED
SHANK

MARKED
SHANK

MARKED
TAPERED
SHANK

FLATTED
SHANK

KNOBBED
SHANK

KIRBED   STRAIGHT   REVERSED

HOLLOW
POINT

CURVED IN
POINT

SUPERIOR
POINT

DUBLIN
POINT

KNIFE EDGE
POINT

SHANK CROSS SECTIONS

FORGED

REGULAR

MUSTAD HOOK TERMINOLOGY

The temper of a hook is a very important consideration and is usually a compromise, with the steel made hard enough to resist straightening but soft enough to give a bit so that it doesn't snap or break. Cheap hooks may vary in temper, some being too soft so they open or straighten easily, others too brittle so they break under stress. For most fresh- and saltwater fishing for the smaller fish it is best to use a hook that gives a bit and opens rather than being brittle and snapping off. You may lose an occasional good-sized fish that straightens out the hook, but you can usually bend it back into shape and land others. A flexible hook will also bend or open up when it is fouled or snagged on the bottom, but a brittle hook will break and be useless.

Of course, big-game hooks are made so that they hold a large fish without bending or breaking. Most of the stronger saltwater hooks have a forged or flattened shank, which gives them more strength. At the other extreme are the light wire hooks, best for delicate baits and certain lures, especially when small fish are sought with light tackle.

Hooks come in different finishes, being japanned or lacquered, bronzed, blued, nickel-plated, silver-plated, gold-plated, tinned or cadmium-plated. The cheapest hooks are usually bronzed, blued or coated with black lacquer. For freshwater fishing the bronzed or blued hooks are fine, but in saltwater they soon rust and weaken. Nickel-plated hooks also rust fairly fast in salt water. Gold-plated hooks are excellent for saltwater use but their higher cost leads most saltwater anglers to buy hooks that are tinned or cadmium-plated.

In recent years more and more hooks have been made from stainless steel, especially for saltwater fishing. They are useful in making lures or tying flies with feathers or hair, which are quickly stained or ruined by rusty hooks. Other hooks have been made from nickel-steel alloys. These are also corrosion-proof, but they tend to be somewhat weaker and softer than those made of carbon steel, so they are usually used for small or medium-sized fish.

Hooks are of course made in different sizes. The numbers can be pretty confusing until you learn to visualize the size of the hook

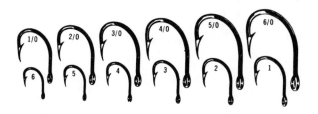

EAGLE CLAW TUNA
AND ALBACORE HOOKS

and the corresponding number. Starting with 22 as one of the smallest hooks made, the numbers increase in size as they proceed down the line to 20, 18, 16 and so on to No. 1. After that they run 1/0, 2/0, 3/0, and up. The largest size is generally 20/0, but there are variations in numbering according to styles or patterns and manufacturers.

Hooks will also vary in weight or thickness of the wire used. Though manufacturers have a standard gauge of wire, called "regular" weight, for each size of hook, hooks may be made of lighter or heavier wire on occasion.

To choose the correct hook for the fish and fishing you plan to do, you must take several things into consideration. There is no such thing as an "all-round" hook. Fish will vary widely in the size, shape and structure of their mouths. They also differ in size, the way they feed, the type of bait or lure they prefer and the way they fight on the end of a line. The size, weight and pattern of the hook you choose will also depend on where you are fishing and the type of fishing tackle, bait and lure you will be using.

ROUND BEND HOOK

Let's examine some of the more popular fresh- and saltwater hooks in more detail so that you can select the right hook for the fishing you plan to do. First on our list is the round bend hook, also called the Gaelic Supreme, Viking or Model Perfect. The round bend's large bite and wide gap allow deep penetration of its hollow point and barb, and it has good holding qualities after a fish is hooked. This hook is widely employed in tying both wet and dry flies and, with longer shanks, in tying streamers and bucktails. It is also a hook to use with live baits where small, sharp-pointed, fine-wire hooks are needed.

The Sproat bend hook has been around for a long time and has been popular for both fresh- and saltwater fishing. A modified round bend hook with a straight point, it hooks well and holds well and is a fine hook if properly made. But it is also turned out for the cheaper markets, and here the materials and workmanship may be inferior. It is a good hook to use with live baits in both fresh and salt water, as well as to tie large wet flies.

The Limerick hook, an old Irish design used in both fresh and salt water for many years, is recognized by its rather sharp, half-round bend, its straight point and heavy wire. It is an effective hook to use with bait or lure for the larger freshwater species and for saltwater fishing. In salt water it is often selected for catching cod and haddock by both sports and commercial fishermen. It is also a good hook for the larger wet flies for trout, bass and salmon. And the long-shank version is popular for streamer flies and bucktails.

SPROAT   CARLISLE   ABERDEEN   LIMERICK

FOUR TYPES OF HOOKS

In recent years the rolled-in point has become a very popular type of hook. The famed Eagle Claw, made by Wright & McGill, and the Beak hook, made by O. Mustad & Son, resemble the claw, talon or beak of a hawk or eagle, hence the names. The rolled-in off-set point on these hooks is supposed to penetrate in the same direction as the pull of the line and thus hook a fish more easily and quickly. The hook's good holding powers make it less likely to be thrown or disgorged. This type is now made in many sizes, styles and finishes for fresh- and saltwater bait fishing and for use on some lures.

EAGLE CLAW HOOKS

The Aberdeen hook, with its almost round bend, is an excellent pattern for light-tackle fishing for small to medium-sized fish with delicate or live baits. Made of fine wire and sharp-pointed, it is not too likely to injure the bait, and the wide gap between point and hook shank facilitate hooking a fish. The light wire enables a live bait such as a minnow to swim or drift more naturally in the water, but has the disadvantage of limiting the hook's use to light tackle and light lines in the pursuit of fairly small fish in fresh and salt water.

The so-called big-bend or wide-bend hook, another hook sometimes used for bait fishing, has a very wide gap, and the bend curves right up on the shank. This allows the fish to engulf the point and barb well inside its mouth. The point of the hook is also in a direct line of pull, giving quick, deep penetration.

Hooks with long shanks, such as the Carlisle and Pacific Bass and Bridgeport Snapper hooks, are used for fish that tend to swallow a bait deep or have sharp teeth that will bite through a leader or line. The long shanks also enable them to hold long, narrow baits, such as worms, minnows, baitfish and strips of fish, more naturally.

Usually long-shanked, too, is the Chestertown or flounder hook, with its narrow bend and narrow gap that make it easier to mouth and swallow, by flounders, which have small, sucking mouths. When the hook is swallowed deep, the long shank makes removal easier. And you can run a sea worm bait up on the long hook shank so that it isn't stolen by fish too readily.

The specialized Virginia and Sheepshead hooks are used mostly for blackfish or tautog and for sheepshead. Heavy wire hooks with short points and barbs, they can penetrate the tough jaws of these fish and withstand their strong, crushing teeth.

The Siwash or salmon hook has long been popular with commercial Pacific salmon fishermen. But it has been adopted by sports anglers going after salmon, bluefish, striped bass and other fish. The strong Siwash hook, made of fairly heavy wire, has a big round bend and a short shank. Its extra-long, narrow, very sharp point penetrates deeply, so it is an excellent hook for fish with tough

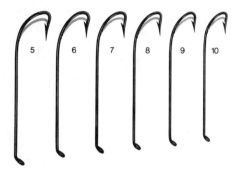

CHESTERTOWN HOOKS

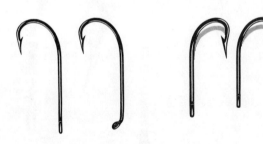

VIRGINIA   SHEEPSHEAD

TWO SPECIALIZED SALT-WATER HOOKS

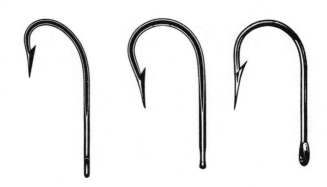

O'SHAUGHNESSY   TARPON   SALMON

THREE POPULAR SALT-WATER HOOKS

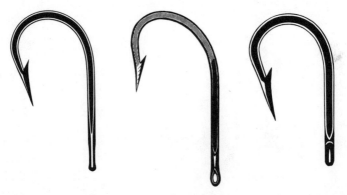

SOUTHERN   SEA DEMON   SEA MATE
AND TUNA

THREE TYPES OF BIG-GAME HOOKS

cartilaginous mouths. This long point also tends to hold leaping fish more securely, with less chance of the hook being thrown.

One of the most popular hooks for saltwater fishing is the venerable O'Shaughnessy, the nearest thing to an all-round saltwater hook. It has a bend similar to that of the Sproat, but it is usually made from heavier wire and the entire hook is forged or flattened to give it extra strength. In addition to its suitability for many salt-water fish, from the smallest to the biggest, it is useful in catching the bigger freshwater species, too, and is the basis for many artificial lures, such as metal squids, jigs and spoons, as well as natural baits rigged for trolling.

When it comes to offshore trolling or big-game fishing, one of the most widely used hooks is the Pflueger Sobey, of heavy forged-wire construction, which has an extreme round bend, an in-point and a needle eye. Another popular Pflueger hook is the Martu, whose diamond out-point ensures quick and deep penetration. O. Mustad makes several fine hooks for big-game fishing, such as the Sea Demon, Sea Master, Tarpon and Tuna and Giant Tuna patterns. Many of these strong hooks are also suitable for shark fishing.

Some rigs call for double or treble hooks both for natural baits or for lures, such as spinners, spoons and plugs. The small, light-wire double and treble hooks are best for freshwater fishing. But for salt water you need the stronger treble hooks made from heavy wire.

Hooks can be bought loose by the dozen, in small packs or boxes, or by the hundred in larger boxes. If you do a lot of fishing and plan to tie many rigs, you're better off buying in quantity. A box of 100 hooks is relatively cheap when you figure out what each hook costs. They are of course much more expensive when bought in smaller quantities. Another reason for buying larger amounts is that you will then have new hooks to replace the old ones. It doesn't pay to take chances with weak or rusty old hooks and possibly lose a big fish.

Choosing the right size and pattern of hook for a specific fish you are going after means you have to consider the fish's mouth structure and size and the size of the fish itself, as well as the patterns recommended by expert anglers for each fish. Here we will list the most popular fish caught in fresh and salt water and the corresponding hook sizes and patterns. When several sizes are listed for the same species, selection depends on the size of the fish sought and the kind of bait used. Small, delicate baits usually require smaller hooks than big, bulky ones. Also the hooks listed below include most of the sizes suited to lures as well as natural baits.

Freshwater Fish

Atlantic Salmon: No. 12 to 5/0 Limerick and Model Perfect or Round Bend hooks for wet flies. No. 12 to 2 Round Bend for dry flies.

Landlocked Salmon: No. 6 to 2/0 Limerick for wet flies and streamers. No. 12 to 8 Model Perfect or Round Bend for dry flies.

Coho Salmon: No. 2 to 4/0 O'Shaughnessy, Eagle Claw or Sproat for lures and baits.

Steelhead: No. 12 to 2/0 Limerick, Model Perfect or Round Bend for nymphs, wet flies and streamers. For dry flies, No. 20 to 6 Model Perfect or Round Bend hooks. For bait fishing, Round Bend, Sproat or Eagle Claw hooks in sizes No. 12 to 1/0.

Trout: All species. No. 4 to 18 Limerick, Model Perfect or Round Bend for nymphs and wet flies. For dry flies, No. 6 to 20 Round Bend hooks. For bait fishing, Round Bend, Sproat or Eagle Claw sizes No. 12 to 1/0.

Lake Trout: No. 1/0 to 6/0 O'Shaughnessy, Sproat and Eagle Claw hooks for bait and lures.

Smallmouth Bass: No. 6 to 2/0 Sproat, Eagle Claw and O'Shaughnessy for bait and lures.

Largemouth Bass: No. 6 to 3/0 Sproat, Eagle Claw and O'Shaughnessy for baits and lures.

Muskellunge: No. 1/0 to 7/0 Sproat, Eagle Claw and O'Shaughnessy for baits and lures.

Pike: No. 1/0 to 6/0 Sproat, Eagle Claw and O'Shaughnessy for baits and lures.

Pickerel: No. 4 to 2/0 Carlisle, Sproat and Eagle Claw for baits and lures.

Walleye: No. 2 to 4/0 Sproat, Eagle Claw and O'Shaughnessy for baits and lures.

Panfish: For bluegills, sunfish, yellow perch, white perch, white bass and crappies, hooks will range from No. 12 to 4 in Sproat, Aberdeen and Eagle Claw for bait and lures.

Bullhead and Catfish: No. 1 to 7/0 O'Shaughnessy, Sproat and Eagle Claw, with the smaller hooks for bullheads and small catfish and the larger sizes for big catfish.

Carp: No. 4 to 3/0 Eagle Claw, Sproat or O'Shaughnessy, depending on size of bait used and size of fish sought.

Saltwater Fish

Striped Bass: No. 1/0 to 9/0 O'Shaughnessy, Eagle Claw and Siwash.

Channel Bass: No. 3/0 to 9/0 O'Shaughnessy, Eagle Claw and Sealey Octopus.

Black Drum: No. 3/0 to 8/0 O'Shaughnessy and Eagle Claw.

Bluefish: No. 3/0 to 8/0 O'Shaughnessy, Eagle Claw and Siwash. For the smaller snapper blues, the Bridgeport Snapper or Carlisle hook in sizes No. 5 to 1.

Common Weakfish: No. 2 to 5/0 Sproat, Eagle Claw or O'Shaughnessy.

Spotted Weakfish: No. 1 to 4/0 Eagle Claw or O'Shaughnessy.

Atlantic Mackerel: No. 1 to 2/0 Sproat, O'Shaughnessy or Eagle Claw.

Spanish Mackerel: No. 2/0 to 4/0 O'Shaughnessy or Eagle Claw.

King Mackerel: No. 4/0 to 7/0 O'Shaughnessy or Eagle Claw.

Bonito: No. 2/0 to 6/0 O'Shaughnessy.

Atlantic Sailfish: No. 5/0 to 8/0 O'Shaughnessy or Sobey.

Pacific Sailfish: No. 7/0 to 9/0 O'Shaughnessy or Sobey.

White Marlin: No. 5/0 to 9/0 O'Shaughnessy or Sobey.

Striped Marlin: No. 7/0 to 12/0 O'Shaughnessy or Sobey.

Blue Marlin: No. 10/0 to 14/0 Sobey, Martu, Sea Demon or Sea-mate.

Swordfish: No. 9/0 to 14/0 Sobey, Sea Demon or Martu.

Bluefin Tuna: No. 8/0 to 14/0 Sobey, Seamate, Sea Demon or Tuna patterns for big fish. No. 6/0 to 9/0 O'Shaughnessy or Sobey for school tuna. No. 2 or 4 Tuna and Albacore style Eagle Claw hooks for live bait for school tuna.

Sharks: No. 9/0 to 16/0 Sobey, Martu, Sea Demon, Sea Master or the Special Shark hooks.

Dolphin: No. 4/0 to 8/0 O'Shaughnessy.

Pacific Yellowtail: No. 1, 2, 4 or 6 short-shank O'Shaughnessy or the Eagle Claw Tuna and Albacore pattern.

Pacific Albacore: No. 1, 2, 4 or 6 short-shank O'Shaughnessy or the Eagle Claw Tuna and Albacore pattern.

Jewfish: 9/0 to 14/0 O'Shaughnessy or big-game hooks.

California Black Sea Bass: No. 8/0 to 14/0 O'Shaughnessy or big-game hooks.

Grouper: No. 4/0 to 12/0 O'Shaughnessy, depending on the species and how big they are running.

Snapper: No. 2 to 9/0 O'Shaughnessy or Eagle Claw, depending on species and size.

Cod and Pollock: No. 5/0 to 9/0 Sproat, Eagle Claw or O'Shaughnessy.

Blackfish: No. 10 to 2 Virginia or No. 2 to 3/0 Eagle Claw.

Sheepshead: No. 3 to 1 Sheepshead pattern or No. 1 to 3/0 O'Shaughnessy or Eagle Claw.

Porgy: No. 4 to 2/0 O'Shaughnessy, Sproat or Eagle Claw.

Sea Bass: No. 1 to 4/0 Sproat, O'Shaughnessy or Eagle Claw.

Croaker: No. 4 to 3/0 Sproat, Eagle Claw or O'Shaughnessy, depending on species and size.

Greenling: No. 4 to 1 Sproat, Eagle Claw or O'Shaughnessy.

Fluke or Summer Flounder: No. 2/0 to 6/0 Carlisle, Pacific Bass or long-shank Eagle Claw.

Winter Flounder: Chestertown No. 12 to 7 or long-shank Eagle Claw No. 8 to 1.

Eel: No. 6 to 1/0 Carlisle or other long-shank hooks.

Northern and Southern Whiting: No. 2 to 1/0 O'Shaughnessy, Sproat or Eagle Claw.

Rockfish: No. 1 to 5/0 O'Shaughnessy or Eagle Claw, depending on species sought.

Saltwater Perch: No. 6 to 1 Sproat, O'Shaughnessy or Eagle Claw.

5. LEADERS

A leader is a connecting length between the fishing line and the lure or hook, or between the snap or swivel and the end of the line. Leaders can be heavier and stronger than the main fishing line to take more shock, wear and tear. They add strength to the terminal tackle, where the teeth, jaws, fins, tails and gill covers of fish can cut a light line. (Some fish, such as sharks, have a sandpaperlike skin that can cut or wear through a line or leader.) Leaders also offer some protection against abrasion from rocks, sand, coral, barnacles, mussels, oysters and underwater obstructions.

The end of the line is also subject to more strain in casting, bottom fishing or trolling, as well as in beaching or boating a fish. Thus a strong leader helps you land more fish.

On the other hand, in fishing for fish that are line- or leader-shy, a thinner and weaker leader may be needed to obtain bites or strikes —a leader that tests less than the main fishing line can be less visible to the fish, as in the case of fly-fishing leaders. But modern monofilament leaders make it possible to have strong leaders that are also less visible.

When choosing the leader you usually have to compromise, but as a general rule your leader should be just heavy and strong enough for the fishing tackle being used and the fish being sought. Leaders that are too thick and heavy frighten fish, tend to kill the action or movement of the lure or bait and are also stiffer and harder to handle.

For freshwater fly fishing you need a leader that keeps the fly away from the thick, heavy fly line and makes the connection less visible. A fly-fishing leader also presents the fly more delicately, with less splash, and enables the angler to work his flies more naturally.

The shorter, level leaders of uniform diameter can be used for bait fishing or when trolling a fly, but for casting and fishing with flies, a long, properly tapered leader is needed to turn over and drop the fly gently on the water. The extreme end, or tippet, of a fly leader is usually the thinnest and weakest part, ranging from 0X to 7X in size.

The strength, length and weight of the leaders you use with fly-fishing tackle will depend on many factors, such as the clearness of the water, the wind, the time of day, the size of the fly and the wariness of the fish. Fly leaders usually measure from 7 1/2 to 12 feet, but longer lengths are available for special fishing conditions. You can buy commercially tied fly leaders, either knotless or knotted. These usually require some modification, however, such as the addition of a heavier butt section or a tippet of the strength you want or need. Most expert fly fishermen prefer to tie their own leaders and buy special stiff and soft monofilament leader material in coils for the purpose.

For freshwater spinning or bait-casting, a shock leader is often necessary. The thin monofilament lines used with spinning or bait-casting outfits are a great advantage since they give you distance even with light lures. They are also less visible, fool wary fish and bring more bites and strikes. So when fishing for small or medium-sized fish in open waters free from obstructions, many anglers simply tie or attach their hook or lure directly to the fishing line.

However, the thin monofilament lines cannot take much abrasion along the first few feet. Constant casting of lures often weakens a line where it rubs against the tip guide. If too heavy a lure is used or your timing is off or your reel holds back the line, the shock of casting may break the line. The thin lines also can't stand much rubbing against rocks, tree trunks, logs or other obstructions. Then you also have the strain of landing or boating a fish from shore or a boat. You often have to stop or hold a fish from running under a boat or around the motor. Or you may have to partially drag a fish in shallow water or along the ground. In some spots you may even have to lift a fish from the water.

So a shock leader at the end of a light fishing line can help you land or boat more fish and prevent the loss of a big fish. It will also save you lures and rigs. Such a monofilament leader can be added quickly in front of a fishing line. It can be a few pounds stronger than the main fishing line, and should be sufficiently long so that a few turns of the leader are on the reel spool when you are ready to cast. This, of course, will vary and will depend on the length of your rod and the distance your lure hangs from the rod tip.

When braided line is used on a bait-casting outfit, a monofilament leader is a must. The braided line is highly visible, and it can't take as much wear and tear as the mono. Here you can choose a monofilament leader of the same strength as the line or a few pounds stronger. When using monofilament line on your bait-casting reel you can add a heavier shock leader up front.

Many anglers like to utilize wire leaders in casting for such sharp-toothed fish as pike or muskellunge, selecting either a single-strand stainless steel or a nylon-covered cable-wire leader. The leader can be anywhere from a few inches to a couple of feet long for casting. But when trolling you can use somewhat longer leaders, going three or four feet.

Even longer leaders may be required when trolling for coho salmon or lake trout. They can be monofilament leaders, running anywhere from four or five feet up to ten or twelve feet in length.

Leaders are just as important in saltwater as in freshwater fishing, perhaps more so. Many saltwater species are line-and-hook shy, and light leaders are a big help in getting bites or strikes. Since saltwater fish often run big, a heavier leader is an aid in landing or boating them. And fishing lines are always being frayed, worn and cut on rocks, coral, barnacles, mussels, oysters and other hazards.

When bottom fishing with heavy monofilament lines such as 30- to 60-pound test, you usually don't need a heavier leader on the end of your line or in the rig itself, unless the bottom is rough with rocks or coral.

Some saltwater bottom fishermen like to use lighter leaders to hold the hook or sinker on their rigs. If these are weaker than the main fishing line, they will break before the line does and thus save part of the rig. And when fishing for wary fish such as snappers, weakfish, striped bass and others, you can use a longer leader that suspends or holds the bait or lure away from the rest of the rig.

When casting in salt water with spinning or bait-casting outfits, for most fish you can use shock leaders of monofilament line a few pounds heavier than the main fishing line. A few turns of the shock leader line should remain on the reel spool when you are ready to cast.

When you fish for bluefish, snook, barracuda, king mackerel, Spanish mackerel and others with sharp teeth or gill covers, you can attach a short wire leader. This can be either single-strand wire or cable wire and should be just long enough to clear the rod tip when you are ready to cast.

Some of the longest and strongest shock leaders are used by surf anglers wielding the longer surf rods. These leaders will run from 10 to 20 feet, depending on the rod used. Surf fishing along sandy shores, rocks, barnacles, mussels and other obstructions is tough on the first few feet of line. The casting itself is also hard on the line, especially with heavy lures. With a shock leader you will save a lot of lures that would break off the lighter spinning line. The shock leader will also take the strain off the first few feet of line when you get a fish close to the beach, rocks or a jetty, and it will help you beach a big fish in a heavy surf. And when fishing from a high jetty you can often lift small fish or drag them up a sloping rock or boulder.

With surf-spinning tackle, monofilament shock leaders anywhere from a few pounds up to 20 or 30 pounds heavier than the main fishing line can be used. If you fish with artificial lures and do a lot of casting, this shock leader need be only about 10 or 15 pounds stronger than the main fishing line. When fishing on the bottom with bait, you can choose a shorter shock leader testing up to 60 pounds.

In casting lures with a surf-spinning outfit, the shock leader should run from the lure to the reel spool with allowance for a few turns to be wound on the spool.

A shock leader is even more necessary with conventional surf tackle, a revolving-spool reel and braided nylon or Dacron line. Since braided line is more visible than mono and it wears and chafes more readily on the end, you can add a shock leader testing a few pounds more than the braided line. Here again this leader should be long enough so that a few turns can be wound on the reel spool.

A good knot for connecting the main fishing line to the shock leader is the surgeon's knot (see next chapter). On the end of the shock leader you can attach a strong snap swivel for quick changing of lures.

If you plan to fish for sharks in the surf, a stainless-steel or cable-wire leader from three to four feet up to eight or ten feet can be used. The shorter lengths can usually be cast as they are, but the longer ones can be coiled and either taped lightly or tied with weak cord or soft wire so that they can be cast more easily. But if sharks are around when you are fishing for other species and you don't want to waste valuable fishing time fighting them, you can use a monofilament leader to hold your hook and bait. A hooked shark will usually bite through the leader. Then you can tie on a new rig and continue fishing for your channel bass or other fish.

For saltwater fly fishing you need leaders of sufficient length, taper and stiffness to cause the fly to turn over at the end of the cast. And the leader should be balanced with the fly line being used. When tying your own fly leaders, you'll find the medium-stiff mono-filament is best. Tapered leaders from 9 to 16 feet can be used for cautious fish such as bonefish, permit, snapper, bonito, snook and striped bass. But for most saltwater fish a shorter 3- to 6-foot leader will suffice. This is made up of three parts—a butt section, a tippet and a shock leader. The butt section will consist of heavy 30- or 40-pound-test mono, the tippet will range from 6 to 15 pounds and the shock leader will be from 60- to 80-pound test.

Saltwater anglers who troll inshore for such fish as striped bass, channel bass, weakfish, snook, tarpon, Pacific salmon and others found close to shore chiefly employ monofilament leaders. However, if they are seeking bluefish, barracuda, king mackerel, Spanish or cero mackerel and other fish with sharp teeth, they may use wire leaders.

The invisibility and flexibility of monofilament leaders make them very effective for most saltwater inshore fish, especially the more wary, harder-to-fool species. The bait or lure floats, rises and sinks or works more naturally too. Anglers trolling for striped bass use mono leaders from 5 or 6 feet up to 30 feet behind a trolling weight. These can test anywhere from 30 to 60 pounds, depending on the caution of the fish, their size and the clearness of the water. Mono leaders can also be attached at the end of wire lines for deep inshore trolling.

In recent years more and more anglers trolling offshore, even for the bigger billfish, have been turning to monofilament leaders. Those testing from 50 to 150 pounds can be used for the smaller fish caught offshore, such as school tuna, albacore, dolphin, sailfish and white marlin. But if you are after the bigger blue marlin, swordfish and giant tuna, mono leaders testing from 200 to 400 pounds are needed.

Of the wire leaders available for inshore and offshore saltwater trolling, three kinds are usually used: the single-strand wire, the plain cable wire and the nylon- or plastic-covered cable-wire leader. There are two kinds of single-strand wire leaders—piano-wire carbon steel and stainless steel. The piano wire is slightly stronger than stainless steel in the same diameter, but it rusts and corrodes more readily. The main advantage of single-strand wire leaders is that they are strong, thin and immune to sharp teeth and abrasion.

They are also relatively inexpensive and can be bought in 25-foot or longer coils. Stainless-steel leaders are easy to work with in making up leaders or rigging baits.

The main disadvantage of single-strand wire leaders is that they tend to develop coils or twists or kinks, and a kinked leader is weak and breaks easily. They are also more visible to the fish than monofilament leaders, especially the shiny finishes (in dull gray or coffee colors, they are less visible). Stainless-steel leaders are numbered from No. 2, which tests about 27 pounds, on up to No. 19, which will test about 352 pounds.

To make stainless-steel leaders, attach the wire to a hook, swivel, snap or other hardware by means of a haywire twist, finishing off the twist with straight barrel wraps. Leave a tiny handle on the end of the wire so that you can bend it and snap it off cleanly, leaving no sharp burr.

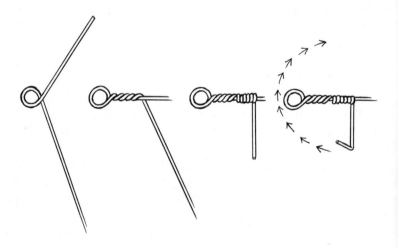

MAKING A HAYWIRE TWIST ON A LEADER

Most of the stainless-steel wire leaders used for inshore trolling run from a couple of feet up to five or six feet. But for offshore trolling, leaders up to 15 and occasionally up to 30 feet are required. A good general rule is to make the leader somewhat longer than the fish you expect to catch.

Cable leader, made of fine twisted stainless-steel strands, is favored for fish that leap or roll or twist in the water when hooked. For sharks it is preferred over the single-strand wire leaders. Some shark anglers use the aircraft-type cable-leader material. You can obtain the plain cable-wire leader material in tests from 18 pounds up to 800 pounds.

You can also use nylon- or plastic-covered cable-wire leaders, which are available in tests from 6 to 210 pounds. They are employed by anglers who do a lot of casting with lures or for bottom fishing or for trolling for the smaller or medium-sized fish. Though they are very flexible, the nylon or plastic material frays or shreds easily or peels off.

To fashion leaders with cable wire you need special crimping pliers or swaging pliers and small brass or copper sleeves or tubes. Loops for attaching snaps, swivels or hooks are made by passing the end of the cable wire through the sleeve until it protrudes a couple of inches on the other side. Next the end of the wire is doubled back through the sleeve to form the loop. The sleeve or tube is then pinched with the crimping pliers in two places to hold the wire firmly inside the flattened tube. When using the cable wire for big fish, some anglers like to attach two sleeves as double insurance.

When tying up rigs for casting, bottom fishing or trolling, pay close attention to your leaders. This terminal tackle is what a fish usually sees, and the kind of leader you choose will determine whether a fish takes your lure or bait or refuses to do so. And the type of leader will also determine whether you land or boat your fish after you hook it.

6. KNOTS

To tie strong, reliable rigs or leaders you must know the best knots for each type. Knots are connections in the line or leader itself, or between two lines, or between leader and line. Knots also attach lures, hooks, sinkers, snaps, swivels and other hardware to the line or leader or some part of the terminal tackle.

A knot is usually the weakest link in your line, leader or rig. Even a good and perfectly tied knot tends to weaken a line, but a wrong knot or a carelessly tied one can weaken your line or leader by as much as 50 percent.

There are many different kinds of knots, but the average angler needs to know only a few basic ones. The main secret in tying good knots is to choose the knot best suited for a particular need, then to form the knot properly and finally to draw it down slowly and snugly so that it doesn't slip. Monofilament, especially in the heavier tests, has a tendency to spring, uncoil and slip. Pliers may be needed to draw such a knot tight.

Practice knot-tying at home until you can perform it quickly and without fumbling. When you have mastered the various steps you will be able to do it almost anywhere—standing in a stream or river, perched on a rock, in a rocking, tossing boat or even at night in a dim light.

IMPROVED CLINCH KNOT

For tying a line or leader to a lure, hook, snap, swivel or other hardware, the improved clinch knot is usually preferred. Running about three or four inches of the end of the leader or line through the eye, double it back and wind it around the standing line for at least five turns. Pass the end through the small opening next to the hook or lure eye, then through the big loop, as shown in the drawing. Now pull the end and slide the turns toward the eye to tighten the knot. Clip off the end.

An alternate knot for tying line or leader to a hook or swivel is the Palomar knot. Here you pass the line through the eye of the hook and return through the eye, making a three- or four-inch loop, as shown. Now hold the line and hook eye with one hand, and with the other hand, tie a loose overhand knot in the doubled line, but do not tighten. Holding the loose overhand knot, pull the loop over the hook or swivel. Then pull on the doubled line to draw the knot up, making sure that the loop doesn't hang up in the hook eye or swivel. Finally pull both line ends to tighten and clip the end about one-eighth inch from the knot.

PALOMAR KNOT

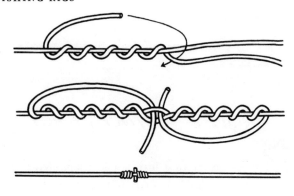

BLOOD KNOT

The blood knot is used to join two lines or leaders when the diameters are about the same or nearly so. Overlap the ends of the lines or leaders several inches, then twist one end around the other, making at least five turns. Place the end between the strands and hold them together with thumb and forefinger. Wind the same number of turns in the opposite direction, using the other end of the line. Now pull on the two ends to draw the turns close together. When they have closed up snugly, pull tight on the ends to make the knot as small as possible. Clip the ends as close to the knot as you can with a nail clipper.

STU APTE IMPROVED BLOOD KNOT

For tying a heavy shock leader to a lighter monofilament line or tippet, the Stu Apte improved blood knot is recommended. Tie the knot the same way as the blood knot, described above, doubling the light line or leader material. Take five turns or twists of the thin line but only three turns of the heavier line.

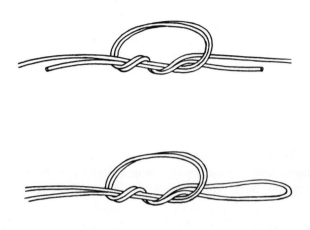

SURGEON'S KNOT

The surgeon's knot is another good method of joining two lines, or leader and line, or adding a shock leader on the end of the line. With this knot you can join different materials in different diameters —for example, a monofilament line and a braided line. It is quick and easy to tie. Simply lay the end of the line and the end of the leader parallel to each other, overlapping them a few inches. Now, holding both lines together, tie a simple overhand knot once, then repeat through the same loop. Each time, of course, you have to pull the leader its entire length through the loop. To finish the knot, grab both ends and pull to tighten it as closely as possible. Clip the ends short so that the knot goes through the guides and winds on the reel spool without catching.

The surgeon's knot can also be used to tie a loop on the end of a leader or line or rig or up on the line or leader to take snelled hooks in making rigs. Here you double the line on the end and tie two overhand knots as shown, tightening the knot. To make a loop for a hook up on the leader or line, you merely form a small loop in the line and tie the two overhand knots.

DROPPER LOOP KNOT

You can also make loops in the middle of your line or leader with the dropper loop knot. Here you make a big loop in the line or leader and wrap the end overhand several times around the rest of the line. Now pinch a small loop at the point marked "X" and thrust it between the turns, as shown by the arrow. Next put a pencil or your finger through the loop to keep it from slipping out and pull on both ends of the line so that the knot will draw up as shown.

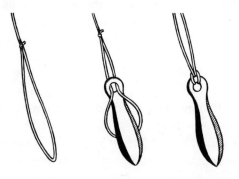

LOOP FOR HOLDING SINKER

A loop on the end of your rig is very handy for changing sinkers. Simply form a big loop by doubling back the line or leader material and tie the surgeon's knot. Then slip on and remove sinkers, as shown in the drawing.

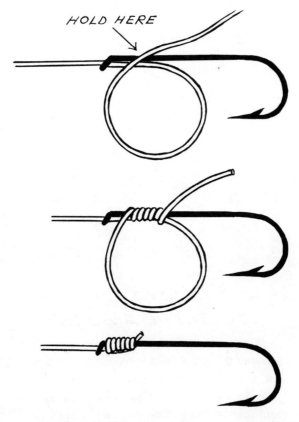

FIRST WAY TO SNELL A HOOK

Every angler who makes up rigs should know how to snell a hook, and one good way to do this is shown here. Pass several inches of monofilament through the turned-down eye of a hook and form a loop. Now pinch this loop between your thumb and forefinger and make five or six turns through the loop and around the hook shank. Holding both lines, close the knot by pulling on the short end of the line. Finish the knot by pulling on the long end of line while holding the hook with the other hand so that the coils slide and tighten against the hook eye.

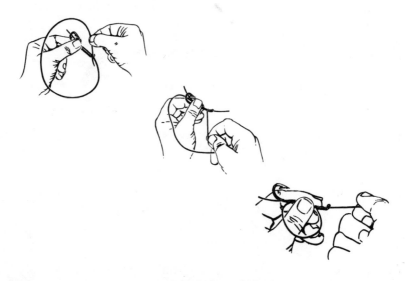

SECOND WAY
TO SNELL A HOOK

Still another way to snell a hook is recommended by the Du Pont company. Cut a leader about six inches longer than the finished snell you want. Pass one end through the hook eye and hold it along the shank of the hook with one hand. Then pass the other end of the leader material through the eye in the opposite direction, extending beyond the eye an inch or two. Hold both sections of the leader along the shank so the leader material forms a circular loop. Take the leg of the loop hanging from the hook eye and, starting at the eye, wind a tight spiral coil of ten or more turns around the hook and the two sections of line you're holding. Shift fingers to hold the coils tightly in place, then pull on the leader end extending from the hook eye. Pull steadily until the entire loop has passed under the coil and out through the eye. Snug up the coils and pull the other end of the leader tight with pliers. Finally, trim off the excess line.

When you practice tying any of the knots described above, hold the drawings in front of you as you follow the various steps. After you have tied the knot dozens of times and on different days, you will no longer need directions or illustrations.

7. FRESHWATER BOTTOM-FISHING RIGS

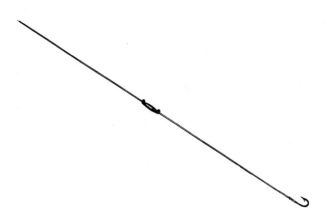

A quick and simple bottom rig for freshwater fishing in shallow water can be made by adding a clincher sinker or several split-shot sinkers a few inches above the hook. Bait the hook and let out enough slack line so that the sinker descends and takes the bait down to the bottom. This rig can be used for trout, bass, bullheads, eels and panfish.

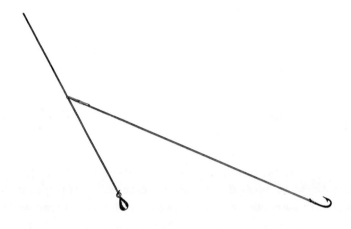

This freshwater bottom rig is versatile in presenting a natural bait for many species. Tie a loop in your line a few inches above the sinker, and tie the hook to this loop on a short 10- or 12-inch snell. A dipsey sinker is then tied a few inches below the hook. Sinkers weighing one-fourth to one ounce can be used for most freshwater fishing, but in rivers with swift currents you may want to use heavier sinkers. This rig can have variations in the height at which the hook is tied, the length of the snell or leader, and the size and pattern of the hook, depending on the fish being sought and the water being fished. This rig can be used in lakes, rivers and ponds, can be cast from the bank or used from a boat. Almost any fish found in fresh water can be caught with it.

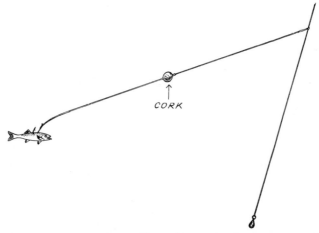

CORK

When you want to present a live minnow in deep water to black bass, walleyes or pike, the rig shown here is a good one. It also keeps the minnow above the weeds or rocks, where it can be seen by the fish. You can tie the small three-way swivel anywhere from three to four feet above the sinker and add a cork in the middle of the leader or a bit closer to the hook. This leader can also be about three or four feet in length. Hook the minnow through the back and lower the rig to various depths.

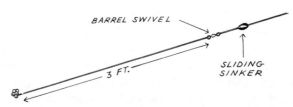

BARREL SWIVEL

3 FT.

SLIDING SINKER

A good rig to use for fishing on the bottom for trout or steelhead with salmon eggs is shown here. Tie to the barrel swivel a three-foot leader with a hook on the end. Then slip a small egg sinker on the line and tie the end to the other eye of the barrel swivel. This rig can be used in still fishing with the bait lying on the bottom or it can be drifted with the current in a stream or river.

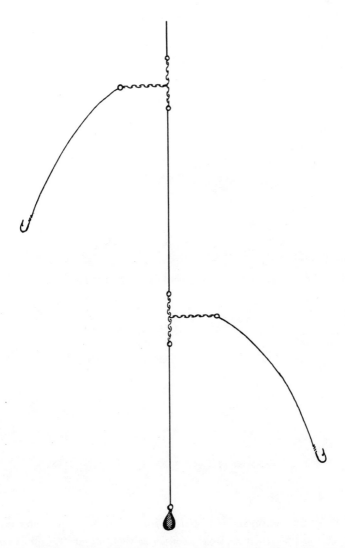

This crappie rig has two wire extension arms that hold the hooks away from the main fishing line, helping to prevent tangles. It can be baited with worms, strips of fish, tiny minnows or any other bait used for crappies.

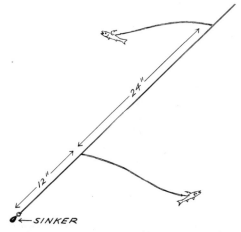

Another good crappie rig for fishing with two tiny minnows is shown here. Tie a sinker on the end of the line and a hook about 12 inches above it. Then tie a second hook about two feet above the first.

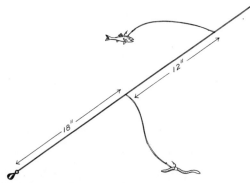

This combination rig can be used for walleyes. Tie a sinker on the end of the line, then a hook on a short snell about 18 inches above the sinker and another hook about 12 inches above the first. Bait the lower hook with a night crawler and the upper hook with a minnow. When you find out which bait the walleyes prefer, you can use that on both hooks.

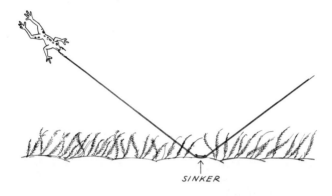

To get a frog down to the bottom, the rig shown here is effective. Use a clincher sinker heavy enough to pull down the frog, adding this about three feet from the hook. Then hook the frog through both lips and let it down to the bottom. If weeds are thick on the bottom you can also add a small cork float about a foot in front of the frog to keep it away from the vegetation.

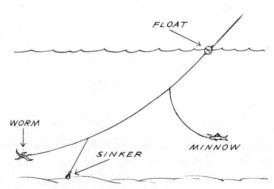

If you want to fish two different baits at different levels with a cane pole and still use a float or bobber to indicate bites, tie up the rig shown. A light sinker will keep the baits down. The float should be adjusted to the depth of the water being fished so that the sinker lies on the bottom and the float is on top.

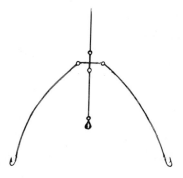

You can often catch yellow perch, white perch and other panfish two at a time by using this two-hook rig. For it you need a short wire spreader with four arms and eyes. The line is tied to one eye. The sinker is tied to the eye just below it, and the two hooks, on short snells or leaders, are tied to the remaining eyes.

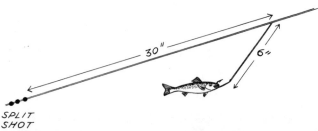

In making this rig, add some split-shot sinkers on the end of your line or leader and tie a 6-inch dropper with a hook about 30 inches above the sinkers. You can add and remove split-shot sinkers as needed. And if they get hung up they will usually slide off and free the rest of the rig. This rig enables you to feel the light nibbles or bites of a fish. It can be baited with a live minnow and be used for walleyes, but it is also effective for many other freshwater species that feed on or near the bottom.

This is a good rig for catching bluegills, bream and other panfish when they are down deep. It makes use of a light one-eighth or one-quarter-ounce sliding sinker on the line, a small barrel swivel to act as a stop and a small hook on a 12-inch leader baited with a worm. This can be cast out and reeled very slowly along the bottom.

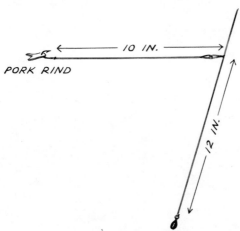

Drifting after bluegills in deeper water—8 to 20 feet—in hot weather, you might like the rig shown here. You can cast it out and retrieve it very slowly. Put a No. 6 hook on the end of a 10-inch leader and a tiny piece of pork rind on the hook.

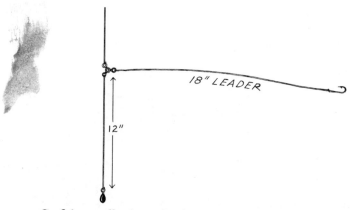

Catfish usually hug the bottom, and your bait should be down there to catch them. For one of the best rigs to use when casting or when fishing a river with a strong current, tie an 18- or 20-inch leader to one eye of a three-way swivel, and attach the sinker about 10 or 12 inches from the other eye. Tie the hook to the end of the longer leader—a 1/0, 2/0 or 3/0 for small catfish and as big as 9/0 for larger specimens.

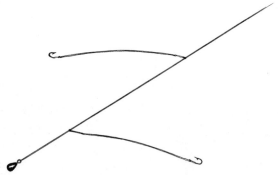

Another good two-hook rig for bullheads or small catfish can be made by tying a dipsey sinker on the end of the line, one hook on a short leader a few inches above the sinker and another hook about a foot above the first.

In fishing a river for catfish, this two-hooked rig can be used. Usually a No. 2 hook is tied on the end and a No. 4 tied about three inches above it; then, about fifteen inches from the hooks, a foot-long dropper loop holding a three- or four-ounce sinker. The two hooks can be baited with shad entrails or other bait, and the rig is let down to the bottom from a drifting boat.

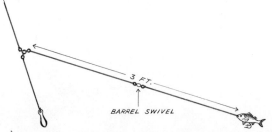

Still another catfish rig is this one used in the Susquehanna River below the Conowingo Dam. It has a three-way swivel, with the fishing line tied to one eye. A three-foot leader with a barrel swivel in the middle is tied to another eye. This holds a double hook on the end and is partly buried in a small fish or a big minnow. The remaining eye holds a dropper with the sinker. The sinker should be heavy enough to hold bottom, but it should move downriver along the bottom with the current when you lift your rod at regular intervals.

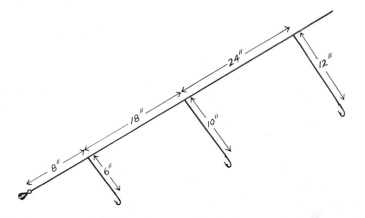

This three-hook rig is used to catch suckers in the spring or any other time they are biting. The first hook, on a 6-inch snell, is tied 8 inches above the sinker. The second hook, on a 10-inch snell, is tied 18 inches above the first hook. And the third hook, on a 12-inch snell, is tied 24 inches above the second hook. The hooks can be baited with small worms.

8. FRESHWATER TROLLING RIGS

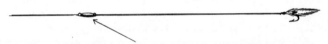

CLINCHER OR RUBBER CORE SINKER

The simplest trolling rig is simply a fly or other lure or bait attached to the end of the line and paid out 20 to 200 feet behind a boat running at a slow to fast speed. This is often done with streamer flies for landlocked salmon. For them you troll rather fast, and you often have to add a clincher or Rubbercore sinker a foot or two in front of the fly to keep it below the surface.

STREAMER

WET FLY

It is often a good idea to troll two flies instead of just one. Tie a bucktail or streamer fly on the end of the leader and a wet fly on a dropper above the streamer. This gives the impression of a minnow or small trout chasing an insect.

73

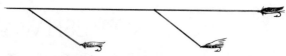

If two flies are effective, three flies may even be more so, especially in trolling for landlocked salmon. The flies can be attached to the main leader on 12- or 14-inch droppers. You can use three different patterns to find out what the prey want. The whole rig looks like a small school of baitfish swimming by and can attract more salmon than a single or double fly.

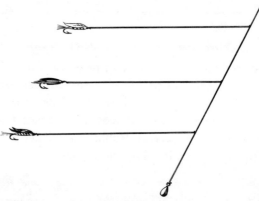

Another use of three flies in trolling for landlocked salmon presents three different streamers or bucktails at varying levels. It gives the fish a choice and also simulates a small school of baitfish or minnows. The sinker on the end allows it to be trolled more deeply by letting out more line.

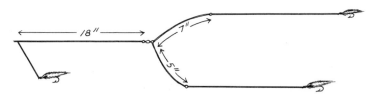

Still another way to troll three-streamer flies for landlocked salmon is with the spreader rig shown here. Form a V-spreader by twisting light stainless-steel wire to make a tiny loop or eye near the center. Before you close this eye, slip on a small barrel swivel. Then form an eye on each arm of the spreader—one arm about seven inches and the other about five inches. Tie leaders of equal length to the two eyes of the spreader and attach two streamer flies. You can then add the third fly, on a short five- or six-inch dropper, to the main leader or line. This can be about a foot and a half in front of the spreader. The upper fly, on the longer arm of the spreader, should be smaller than the other two flies.

Another effective rig for trolling for landlocked salmon is made by tying a streamer fly on a short dropper and then sewing a smelt on the end of the line about three feet behind the fly.

You can also try trolling two minnows for bass, trout, landlocked salmon and other fish. Just take a length of nylon leader material and tie a loop, leaving one strand long and the other somewhat shorter. Tie a hook on each strand and impale a small minnow on the top, or shorter, leader and a larger minnow on the lower, longer, leader. Dead minnows can be used if you are slow-trolling with this rig. But you can also drift in a boat and let out live minnows on both hooks.

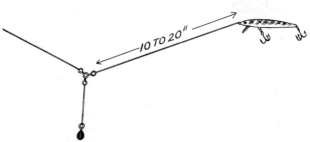

A buoyant underwater plug made of balsa wood or hollow plastic can be used near the bottom with the aid of the rig drawn here. Attach a three-way swivel to the end of your line, add a leader 10 to 20 inches long to one eye of the swivel, attaching the plug to the end of the leader. Then connect a sinker on a short dropper to the other eye of the swivel. This rig can be trolled along the bottom or it can be cast out and reeled in, always slowly. Raise the rod tip quickly to activate the plug, then drop it, allowing the sinker to settle back to the bottom. Keep repeating this at a slow pace as you reel in the slack. The buoyant plug will stay above the rocks and weeds and will foul less than a deep-running or sinking plug. Also, it will have more action at slower speeds than the other plugs or lures.

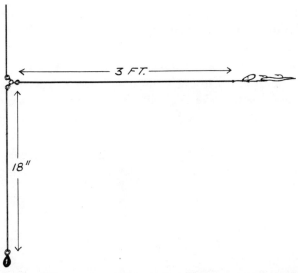

This rig is a good one for slow and deep trolling for walleyes near the bottom in lakes and rivers. Use a June Bug spinner with two hooks on a three-foot leader and tie it to one eye of the three-way swivel. Bait the hooks with either night crawlers, lamprey eels or minnows. The 18-inch dropper line holding the sinker should be weaker than the main line and the leader holding the spinner. Then if the sinker gets fouled or snagged you can break it off and save the rest of the rig. When trolling for walleyes, move the boat slowly and try to feel the sinker bumping bottom so you know that it's deep enough.

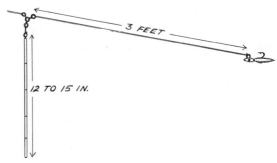

A highly effective rig for trolling for walleyes is made by tying a "pencil" sinker, up to 15 inches long, to one of the eyes of a three-way swivel. This type of sinker is usually made by casting lead around a heavy wire, as from a coat hanger. They can be tied with a weak line that will break if the sinker gets snagged—though its thinness and length make this sinker more snagproof than ordinary sinkers. A three-foot monofilament leader is tied to another eye of the three-way swivel and the lure attached to it. The fishing line is then tied to the remaining eye. This rig works best when trolled slowly in water from 10 to 30 feet deep, especially over rocky bottoms.

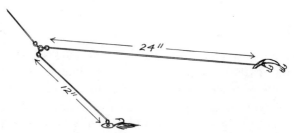

Still another kind of walleye rig is a combination lure type in which a two-foot leader is tied to one eye of the three-way swivel and a light plug of the floating type attached. Then a jig on a shorter 12-inch dropper is tied to the other eye of the swivel, providing the weight to get the lures down and giving the fish a choice of two lures. With its single hook riding up, the jig gets snagged less often, but if it does snag, you can tie it on a lighter line, which will break, saving the plug and the rest of the rig.

KEEL
SINKER

A good walleye rig to use with shallow-running floating plugs employs a short wire leader about eight inches long. Attach the plug to this leader and a keel-type sinker to the other end, then the line. The sinker should be heavy enough to pull down the lure and bump bottom in the current of a river. It can be trolled very slowly along the bottom. Or you can station yourself above a hole where walleyes are found and drift the lure back, bouncing bottom along the way. By letting out line and shifting locations, you can cover the entire hole.

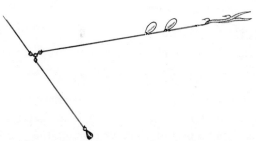

Another walleye rig makes use of a dipsey sinker attached to a three-way swivel. Then a longer two-foot leader has two spinners, with a double hook for such baits as night crawlers, leeches or a minnow. The rig can be trolled slowly along the bottom.

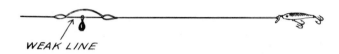

WEAK LINE

This rig is a good one if you don't like to fight a fish with a sinker or trolling weight on the line when deep-trolling with a plug or other lure. Form two loops on your regular fishing line where you want the weight to be, then tie a weaker line, holding a sinker, between the loops. When you hook a fish the weak line will break, freeing the sinker, and you can fight the fish with no weight.

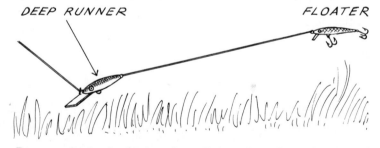

DEEP RUNNER   *FLOATER*

Remove the hooks from a deep-diving plug, then tie a three-foot leader behind it and attach a floating plug. The deep-running plug will go down and bump bottom or move through the weeds without fouling, while the trailing plug will clear the weeds or bottom and bring strikes.

4 TO 6 OZ.
KEEL SINKER

3 TO 4 FT. WIRE LEADER

This muskie or pike rig can be made by tying a four- to six-ounce keel sinker on the end of your line, then tying a three- to four-foot wire leader with the lure on the end to the keel sinker. A spoon, plug or spinner can be the lure. The rig is used for fairly fast trolling on the larger lakes and rivers with a short line. But you can also let out more line or change trolling weights to reach various depths.

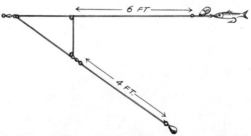

6 FT.

4 FT.

A good deep-trolling rig for lake trout, which makes use of a triangular wire spreader, is illustrated above. Attach a six-foot leader with spinner and minnow to one eye of the triangle, then a dropper four feet long to hold the sinker. The remaining eye holds a barrel swivel to which the fishing line is tied.

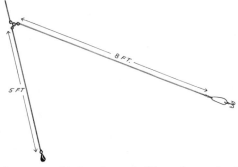

Another lake trout rig for deep trolling along the bottom makes use of a three-way swivel to which an eight-foot leader is tied. This holds the lure, usually a spoon or plug. A five-foot dropper, holding the sinker, is tied to the other eye. This line can be weaker than the main fishing line so it will break if the sinker catches in the rocks. The sinker weight will vary according to the depth you are trying to reach.

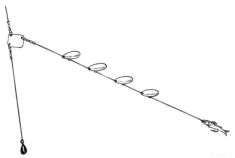

Still another lake trout rig, often called the "cowbells" or "Christmas tree" rig, uses several spinners on a leader ahead of the lure. This is attached to a flat rudder to help prevent line twist. A sinker ranging from three to eight ounces on a dropper is also tied to the rudder. For best results troll this rig with a lead-core or wire line in depths from 50 to 150 feet.

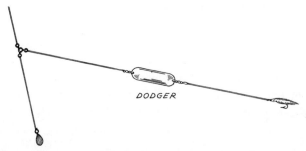

DODGER

This rig is used in trolling for coho salmon. Tie a three-way swivel to the fishing line and then connect a leader with a "dodger," or metal flasher, about three feet from the swivel. Add another couple of feet of leader and attach your lure or bait. Finally, to complete the rig, tie a dropper with a sinker to the remaining eye of the three-way swivel. This rig can be trolled at varied depths, depending on how much line you let out and how heavy a weight you use. To get down even deeper, you can troll it on a wire line.

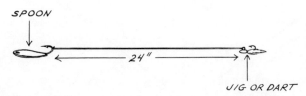

SPOON

24"

JIG OR DART

This lure combination is especially good in trolling for shad. It consists of a tiny spoon tied to the line and a two-foot leader tied to the hook of the spoon. A small white or yellow jig or a shad dart goes on the end of the leader. Though it is used primarily in trolling, this rig can also be cast. And besides white and hickory shad, it will take white perch and white bass.

Also suitable in trolling for white or hickory shad is a light one-eighth- or one-fourth-ounce keel sinker tied about three feet above a tiny silver spoon. This should be trolled very slowly close to the bottom.

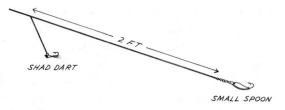

Another good double-lure rig for catching hickory shad has a tiny spoon on the end of the line and a shad dart on a short dropper about two feet in front of the spoon. This can be cast or trolled.

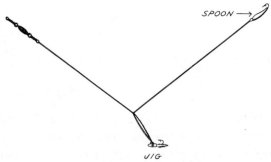

Yet another simple combination rig can be made for trolling for shad. Take about a four-foot length of fifteen-pound-test monofilament line, and forming a loop at the exact center, tie a knot about three or four inches from the end of the loop. Attach a small jig to this loop. Now tie a spoon on one end of this rig and a light trolling weight with bead chain to the other end. The fishing line, of course, is attached to the other eye of the trolling weight.

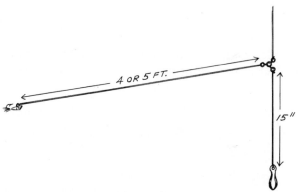

Another shad rig that can be used for trolling in a river is tied with a four- or five-foot leader and a shad dart on the end. The sinker is attached to a fifteen-inch dropper and ranges from one to four ounces, depending on the depth of the water and the strength of the current.

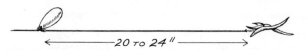

An effective rig for white perch is a tiny gold spinner about 20 to 24 inches ahead of a hook baited with worms. Troll this very slowly at various depths until a school of fish is located. Then troll in the same spot at the same depth.

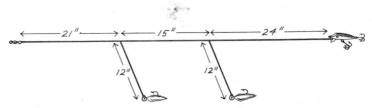

This combination rig is used in trolling deep for white bass. Taking about a five-foot leader, tie a barrel swivel on one end and an underwater plug on the other. Then attach a jig on a 12-inch dropper about two feet in front of the plug, and about 15 inches ahead of that, another jig on a 12-inch dropper. A yellow plug with yellow jigs usually works best, but you can try other colors.

To make a good rig for trolling bait very slowly along the bottom, put a large clincher sinker on the leader or line about three feet ahead of the hook. Then add a small cork several inches from the hook. The hook can be baited with a worm, leech, frog, crayfish or minnow. The sinker will take the bait down to the bottom, but the cork float will keep it above the weeds or rocks. This rig works best for slow trolling, using a small motor or oars, or drifting with a light wind. When you get a bite, give some slack line so the fish has a chance to swallow the bait.

9. OTHER FRESHWATER RIGS

One of the best ways to add weight to a worm rig used for trout is to tie a short three-inch monofilament dropper about a foot above the hook, then pinch split-shot sinkers on the dropper. This enables you to add or remove the shot without damaging the leader. Also, if the sinkers get caught on rocks they will usually slip off the end of the dropper, freeing your rig.

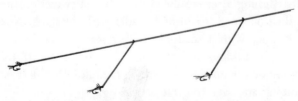

For a change of pace try fishing three nymphs at a time. The combination often attracts and interests trout more than a single nymph would.

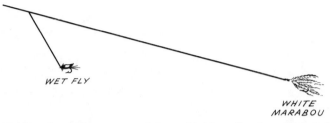

WET FLY

WHITE
MARABOU

In fishing for big trout at night, a highly effective rig consists of a white Marabou streamer tied on the end of your leader, with a large wet fly on a dropper above it. Some fish will hit the Marabou, but others will go for the wet fly.

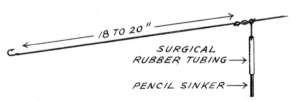

18 TO 20"

SURGICAL
RUBBER TUBING ⟶

PENCIL SINKER ⟶

For drift fishing after steelhead, tie a barrel swivel on the end of the line, then tie an 18- to 20-inch leader with the hook. Next attach a short dropper with a small bit of surgical tubing. Push a pencil sinker into the tubing, and the rig is ready to go. If the sinker gets hung up on the bottom, a yank on the line will pull it out of the rubber tubing and save the rest of the rig.

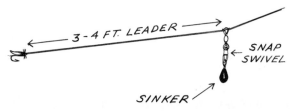

Another steelhead rig, usable with a wide variety of wet flies, streamers, wool yarn, salmon eggs and other baits, has a snap swivel, which makes it easy to change weights to match the currents and depth of the water being fished. The rig is fished by slowly raising and lowering the rod as it bumps bottom, reeling in only when lowering. It has the advantage over a dropper-leader-sinker rig in that it doesn't twist and tangle as often.

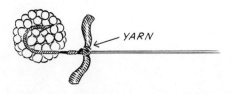

When using steelhead or salmon eggs for steelhead fishing, try tying a short length of fluorescent red or orange yarn on the line just above the hook for added visibility and attractiveness.

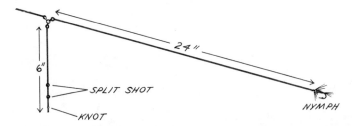

This rig is used with nymphs for Michigan steelhead when they run up streams and rivers to spawn. It consists of a small three-way swivel on the end of a fly leader, to which you attach a two-foot leader with the nymph on the end. Tie a six-inch dropper to the remaining eye and add a split-shot sinker or two, the number depending on the depth fished and the speed of the current.

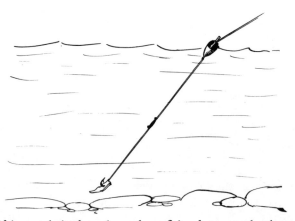

In drifting a bait for channel catfish close to the bottom, the float will keep this rig from hanging up on a rock or log and will give the bait some movement too. Add a small clincher sinker on the leader to keep the bait down in the current.

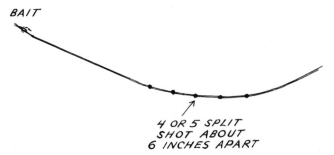

With natural baits such as stonefly nymphs, larvae, grasshoppers, crickets, salmon eggs and worms used in a stream for trout or bass, this rig is a good one. It distributes the split-shot sinkers along the leader about six inches apart and enables a bait to drift naturally near the bottom.

A small jig can be worked in shallow water over a weed bed without getting hung up if it is attached below a float or cork. Measure the water depth over the weed bed and set your float a few inches short of it. For best results, move the jig very slowly in short jerks and pauses.

This combination rig with a Marabou streamer up front and a small wet fly trailing about five or six inches behind is good for trout. A great attractor fly, the Marabou draws out the big trout, which will then hit the wet fly.

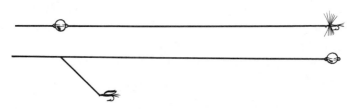

The two rigs shown above enable the angler using spinning or spin-casting tackle to cast dry flies, wet flies, nymphs, streamers and bass bugs a good distance. In the first, the plastic bubble float is tied about three feet in front of the fly. In the second, the fly is put on a short dropper about three feet ahead of the bubble, which is tied on the end of the line.

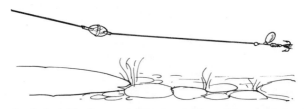

The plastic bubble float can also be used to fish a weighted spinner deep near the bottom without hanging up too often. Add one of these floats about a foot or so ahead of the spinner. Fill the float with enough water to sink it and then reel it slowly along the bottom to catch trout, bass and walleyes.

For river shad, this rig can be used with a fly rod or ultra-light spinning rod. It consists of red, yellow, orange or silver beads in front of a No. 1 plain hook and a split shot or two on the leader above the hook. It is important to let beads and hook sink close to the bottom and then retrieve the rig in a rise-and-sink action.

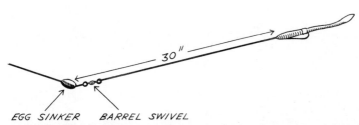

A highly effective rig to use with a plastic worm when the bass are down in water from 20 to 40 feet deep is shown here. Thread a sliding egg sinker on your line, then tie a small barrel swivel on the end, to which you attach a 30-inch leader and the hook. Use a thin wire hook and a floating worm, which will keep it off the bottom.

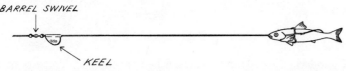

In using a sewn minnow that is rigged to wobble in the current of a stream or river, it's a good idea to add a small transparent keel and barrel swivel about two feet above the bait. This will help to prevent line twist but will not hamper the action of the minnow. You can employ this rig for big trout, bass and walleyes.

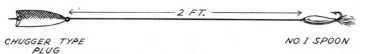

CHUGGER TYPE
PLUG

NO. 1 SPOON

Take a chugger-type surface plug and remove the hooks. Behind
the plug add a two-foot monofilament leader testing about eight
pounds. Then attach a small spoon with feathers to the end of the
leader. The rig that results can be used for both smallmouth and
largemouth bass.

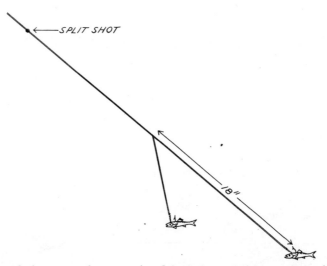

A good rig to use for crappies fished through ice consists of two
No. 8 hooks, one on the end of the line and the other tied about 18
inches above. Both hooks are baited with tiny minnows, and to get
them down deep enough you can add some split shot or a small
clincher sinker about a foot above the bottom hook.

Remove the treble hook from a small spoon and tie a six- to eight-inch length of monofilament and a tandem hook on the end. Then add a night crawler or big worm on each of the hooks. This rig can be trolled or cast for trout or bass.

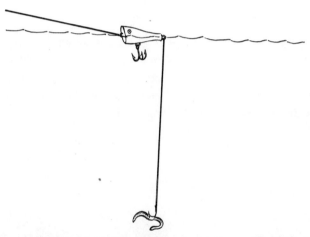

You can fish with a lure and a natural bait at the same time. Get a small surface plug such as a popper and remove the tail treble hook. Tie a short 12- or 15-inch leader and a bait hook to the eye in the tail of the plug. Then bait the hook with a worm or other bait. The plug will provide casting weight and can also be twitched or popped lightly to attract attention to the bait. Most of your fish, such as panfish, will be caught on the live bait, but every so often a bass may decide to sock the plug instead.

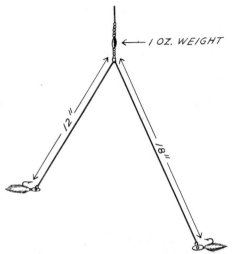

This is a good rig to use in jigging straight up and down in deep water for bass or walleyes. Use a one-ounce lead bead chain sinker on the end of your line and then attach two leaders—12 inches and 18 inches. Then add a one-eighth-ounce jig on the short leader and a three-eighths-ounce jig on the longer one.

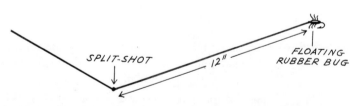

For catching big bluegills when they are down deep, tie a small floating foam-bodied bug with rubber legs on the end of the leader. Add a one-eighth- or one-fourth-ounce split-shot sinker about a foot above the bug. To use this rig, cast it out and let it sink to the bottom, then retrieve it very slowly.

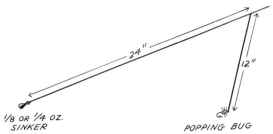

Another good rig to use for bluegills when they are down deep is shown here. Tie a small one-eighth- or one-fourth-ounce sinker on the end of your line. About two feet above the weight, attach a 12-inch dropper to which you tie a small cork-bodied popping bug with rubber legs. Cast this out and when the sinker hits bottom retrieve it slowly, giving the bug some action with light twitches of the rod.

When bluegills are feeding on top, use a plastic bubble float with a 12- or 14-inch leader tied behind it, a small panfish bug or bushy dry fly on the end of the leader. Cast this toward shore or some lily pads and work it back slowly, alternately twitching the rod tip and resting.

You can quickly make this spinner-worm combination for panfish. Take a small weighted spinner and remove the treble hook. Then add a short eight- to ten-inch nylon leader behind the spinner and tie on a small hook. Baiting this with a small worm, cast it out and reel it back slowly at various depths, until the fish are located.

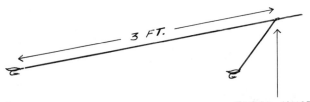

BLOOD KNOT

In using two wet flies, the quickest way to make a dropper strand for the higher fly is to tie a blood knot. But pull out about seven or eight inches of the heavier leader end while tying the knot. Then attach your wet fly to the end of this dropper. The distance between the two flies should be about three feet.

A tricky way to cast a plastic worm, get it down to the bottom fast and work it deep is to attach it on a short leader behind a jig. The same idea will work with other lures and even natural baits.

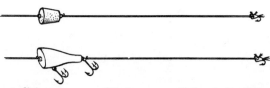

Because small bugs or panfish bugs are light, it is difficult to cast them in a spinning or casting outfit for small panfish. This problem can be solved with a small weighted cork float or a small surface plug ahead of the panfish bug, as shown in the drawing. Use a nylon leader about 15 inches long to tie the small panfish bug to the lure or cork.

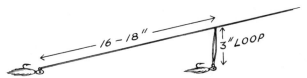

Two jigs on the end of a line often work better than one. Tie a loop about 16 or 18 inches from the end of the line and attach a jig to it; then tie a second jig on the end of the line. This rig can be trolled slowly or cast and bumped along the bottom. Bass, pickerel and panfish will go for it, and you'll often hook two fish at a time.

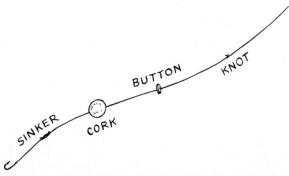

When a bobber or cork float is too high up on the line, it makes for difficult casting. This problem can be solved easily with a sliding float rig. Simply tie a knot on your line with a short, separate piece of cord at the spot where the bobber or float should stay. Slip a button on the leader or line, then the float or bobber, then a small clincher sinker, and finally tie on the hook. The float will slide down to the sinker when you cast, but will move back to the knot when at rest in the water. Make certain that the hole in the float is big enough for the line to move through freely.

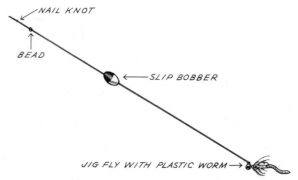

Another sliding bobber rig has a plastic worm and jig on the end that is deadly for smallmouth bass. It consists of a jig fly with black head and black Marabou feathers and a short three-inch plastic worm on the hook. A nail knot is tied so that the rig can slip up and down on the main fishing line. Then thread a bead on the line below the knot and add a bobber or float that slips freely up and down the line. The depth of the bobber will depend on where you are fishing. Usually best results are obtained in fairly shallow water, with the jig and worm just off the bottom or touching bottom.

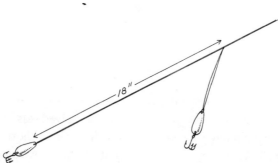

A good rig to use in jigging for lake trout through the ice is made up with two spoons. One spoon is tied to the end of the line, while the other is tied to a dropper about 18 inches above the first spoon. Strips of smelt on the hooks make the spoons even more attractive.

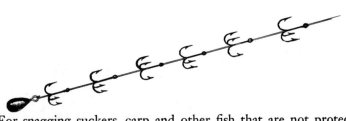

For snagging suckers, carp and other fish that are not protected from this method, tie up to six or more treble hooks about three inches apart above a sinker. Then lower or cast the rig out and jerk it fast and hard through a school of fish to snag them.

10. SALTWATER BOTTOM-FISHING RIGS

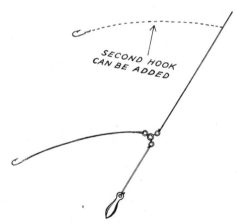

SECOND HOOK
CAN BE ADDED

This basic bottom rig is used by many saltwater anglers fishing from party boats, private boats, rowboats, piers, docks, bridges, jetties—anywhere where bottom fish are caught. A single-hook bottom rig is made by simply tying the snelled hook to the main fishing line a few inches above the sinker. You can tie it directly to the line or use a three-way or cross-line swivel or some kind of spreader to help keep the hook away from the fishing line. To make a two-hook bottom rig, just add another hook above the first one. Of course, in these basic bottom rigs your choice of hook size and pattern, type of sinker and length of leaders or snells will depend on the fish you are seeking and where you will be fishing. For most fish, snells or leaders a foot or a foot and a half long will be ample. The usual hooks for these rigs will be Sproat, O'Shaughnessy or Eagle Claw. Sinkers will range from about one ounce for shallow water and light tackle up to sixteen ounces or more for deep water, strong tides and heavy tackle. Round, bank and diamond sinkers are customary with these basic bottom rigs.

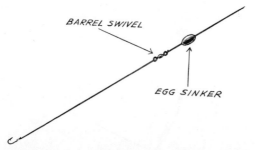

The sliding sinker rig is popular in southern waters for use from drift boats, party boats, small boats, piers and bridges in bottom fishing for various saltwater species. To make it, slip an egg sinker on the line and tie on a barrel swivel, attaching your hook to it on any length leader you desire or need. This is a good rig to use for slow biters or fish that shy away from heavy weights. It lets a fish take line through the hole in the sinker without feeling the weight.

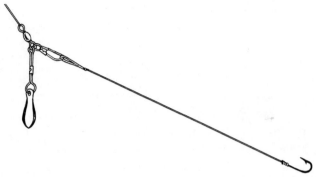

For a rig that can be made up quickly, attach a leader or snell with a hook to a snap swivel. Taking a connecting link with an oversize loop on one end, slip the end with the small loop on the swivel. Then open the oversize loop and put on the sinker. Such a rig can be made up in a matter of seconds, and you can quickly change hooks or sinkers when necessary.

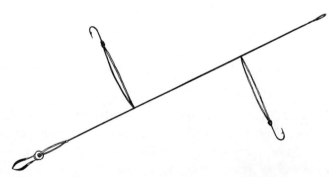

This is a quick no-hardware rig that can be used for many salt-water species. To make it, start with a piece of monofilament about 40 inches long, tying a small loop on one end, to which the fishing line will be attached. Tie a large loop to hold the sinker on the other end. In between attach two dropper loops, to which the hooks are added. Dull or rusty hooks can be replaced quickly on this rig, and sinkers can be changed in a hurry to suit the fishing conditions. Such a rig is inexpensive and is especially suited for fishing in rocky or weedy areas or around obstructions where you get hung up and lose many rigs.

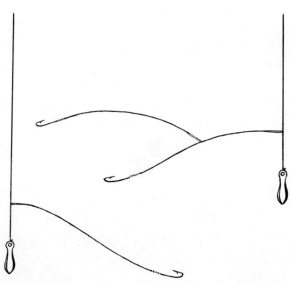

These two rigs, which dispense with the need for most snaps, swivels, spreaders or other hardware, are used for winter flounders. Simply tie a Chestertown hook of the desired size on a foot-long snell a few inches above the sinker. To make a two-hook rig, tie another hook to the snell or leader of the first one at about the middle.

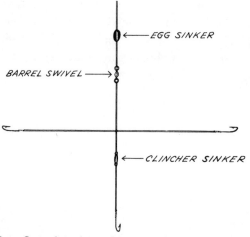

Still another flounder rig makes use of three hooks. After sliding a small egg sinker on your line and tying a barrel swivel on the end of the line, you place three Chestertown hooks crosswise, as shown, and add a small clincher sinker.

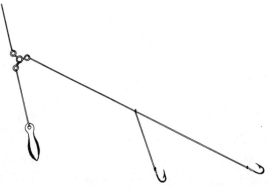

This blackfish or tautog rig is similar to that for two-hook flounder except that the second hook is tied on a shorter snell to the middle of the longer one. Virginia hooks replace flounder hooks, though you can substitute suitable hooks and baits if you are after croakers, sheepshead, porgies, snappers and other bottom feeders. Some of these fish are notorious bait stealers, and with two hooks you'll have to reel in less often. You can also use two different baits, such as a fiddler crab on one hook and a piece of clam on the other.

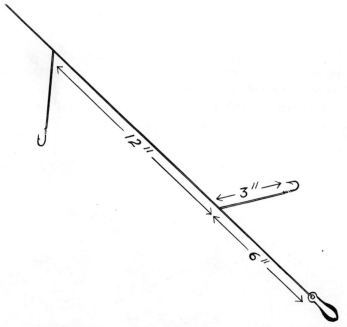

A good porgy rig can be made up of two No. 1/0 hooks on short three-inch snells. Tie the lower hook about six inches above the sinker and the upper hook about twelve inches above the first one. The short snells help prevent the hooks from fouling around the leader or main line.

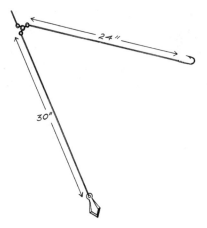

This is the basic one-hook rig used for cod from the party boats along the Atlantic coast, especially over rocky areas or wrecks where lower hooks tend to hang up. However, if you are fishing over sandy or gravel bottoms, you can tie the hook lower and add a second hook about two or three feet above it.

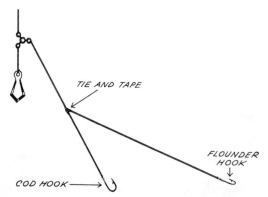

Anglers fishing off Block Island, R.I., often encounter cod and big snowshoe flounders on the same grounds. In order to catch both species with the same rig they use a combination like the one above. The cod hook is tied to the main fishing line just above the sinker, and then the flounder hook is added to the leader or snell of the cod hook. Naturally the cod hook is larger and stronger, usually an O'Shaughnessy or Eagle Claw from 6/0 to 8/0 in size. The flounder hook should be one of the larger Chestertown patterns. The cod hook is baited with a good-sized portion of skimmer clam. The flounder hook can be baited with the stringy lip or mantle of the clam.

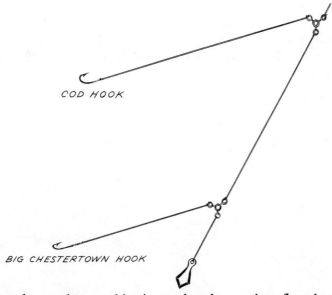

COD HOOK

BIG CHESTERTOWN HOOK

To make another combination cod and snowshoe flounder rig, tie a big No. 4 Chestertown hook a few inches above the sinker. Then about two feet above this hook tie a cod hook on a longer snell or leader. The cod hook can be baited with a half or whole skimmer clam, while the lower hook should be baited with thin slivers of clam for the flounders.

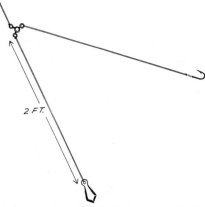

This rig is used for cod, pollock, hake and tilefish in the deeper offshore waters of the Atlantic. Here you tie a No. 7/0 to 9/0 hook on a long snell about two feet above the sinker. You can bait the hook with clams if cod, pollock or hake are running. For tilefish use a small whole squid or cut fish.

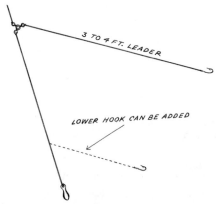

The "high leader" rig is a good one for striped bass, weakfish, bluefish and other active species that often swim and feed off the bottom. Tie the hook anywhere from three to four feet above the sinker on a leader of the same length. The sinker should be heavy enough to hold bottom in the current but light enough to move when lifted. This rig can be baited with a sandworm or a strip of squid, or shedder or soft crab or shrimp or small baitfish, and bounced along the bottom with the tide. After letting the rig out about a hundred feet, with frequent stops in one place, reel back in slowly and repeat the process. You can add another hook on a short snell just above the sinker to catch bottom feeders while waiting for action on the top hook.

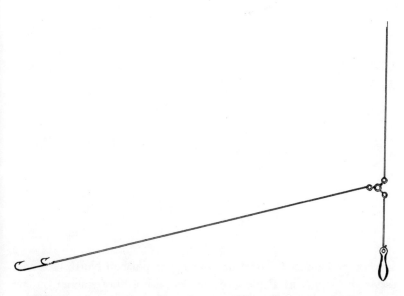

This rig, for summer flounders or fluke, features a leader any-where from two to three feet long. Tie a Carlisle or Pacific Bass long-shanked hook to the end of the leader. Sizes from 3/0 to 5/0 are best for small fish, while 6/0 or 7/0 hooks can be used for the big doormats. To hold the strip of squid or baitfish more securely, many anglers like to add a second, smaller hook near the eye of the larger one and impale the bait on both of them.

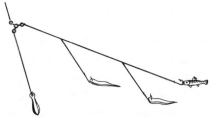

Still another summer flounder or fluke rig is this combination type with three hooks that gives the fish three baits to choose from. Using a three-foot leader, tie one hook on the end and two hooks on short droppers into the leader. You can put a live killie on the end hook, a strip of squid and spearing on another hook and a strip cut from the belly of a fluke or other fish on the remaining hook.

Another summer flounder or fluke rig, popular in North Carolina, uses two long-shank Eagle Claw hooks with a brass spinner on the top hook and a silver spinner on the bottom one. A connecting link holds a dipsey or bell type of sinker weighing two or three ounces. The hooks are baited with strips of fish or small live baitfish. The rig should be worked from a drifting boat, whose movement will activate the spinners. From a bridge or pier it can be let out in a strong tide and then reeled back slowly along the bottom. Or you can cast it out and reel it back, slowly dragging bottom.

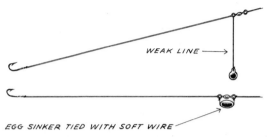

WEAK LINE ⟶

EGG SINKER TIED WITH SOFT WIRE

When fishing on the bottom for tarpon or other game fish that leap or make long, fast runs, or when you want to get rid of the sinker on very light tackle, the two "sinker release" rigs shown here can be utilized. With the top one you tie a barrel swivel on the end of the line, then add leader and hook. Then tie the sinker on a short dropper to one of the barrel swivel eyes. This line should be very weak so that it will break when a fish leaps or runs. The second rig starts off with a barrel swivel and leader and hook, too, but here an egg or oval sinker is tied to the barrel swivel with soft wire. Make only a loose turn or two so it stays on while you fish but comes off when a fish leaps or runs.

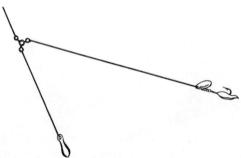

A small spinner with some red beads can be added to the regular bottom rig, as shown above, to attract croakers and other fish. Such a rig is most effective when you drift or you let it out from an anchored boat in a fairly strong tide so that the spinner revolves. It can be baited with sea worms, pieces of clam, shedder crab or shrimp.

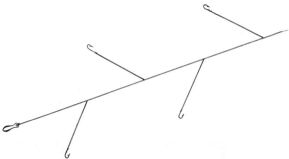

The multiple-hook rig is commonly used for whiting or silver hake in northern waters. Tie Carlisle or Aberdeen hooks in sizes from 2/0 to 5/0 one above the other until you have four or five on your line. Silversides or spearing, sand eels or strips of fish, can be used as bait for the whiting. But the same rig can be used with smaller hooks for smelt, mackerel, herring and other fish that travel in big schools and feed near the bottom. In tying this rig, attach the snells and hooks to the line or leader with loops and knots rather than with hardware.

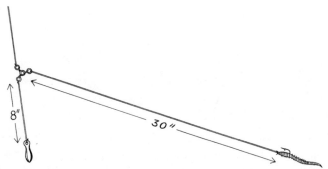

The striped bass drifting rig shown here works well for drifting in a boat in tidal rivers, bays and inlets and off beaches. Tie a small three-way swivel about eight or ten inches above a one- or two-ounce sinker. Then tie a 30-inch leader and a No. 2/0 or 3/0 hook to the swivel and attach your fishing line to the remaining eye of the swivel. Bait the hook with a whole sandworm by running it just through the head.

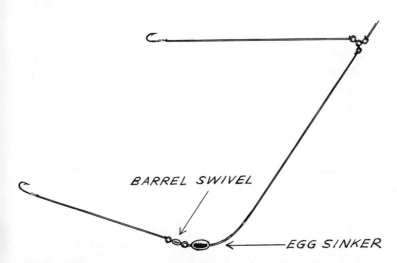

BARREL SWIVEL

EGG SINKER

This rig presents two baited hooks at different levels—one on the bottom and the other about 18 inches above. To tie it, attach your fishing line to one eye of a three-way swivel. Then a short leader and hook is tied to the second eye and a length of leader material to the remaining eye. Slip an egg sinker on this leader and tie a barrel swivel on the end of the line. To complete the rig, tie a second hook to the barrel swivel. Although primarily for croakers, this rig is effective in drifting and fishing for fluke or summer flounders, sea bass, porgies, snappers and other bottom species.

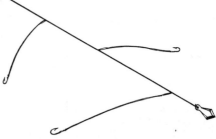

To fish for whiting and cod at the same time, the rig pictured above is the one to use. The two upper hooks can be short 10- or 12-inch snells with 4/0 or 5/0 hooks tied to the ends. The lower hook is on a longer 18- or 20-inch snell and is a larger 6/0 or 7/0 size. The upper hooks can be baited with spearing, strips of squid or fish for whiting. The lower one can be baited with a whole skimmer clam for cod.

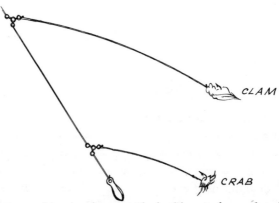

CLAM

CRAB

Another combination bottom rig is this one for cod and blackfish. The top hook, on a long two-foot leader, holds a 6/0 or 7/0 hook baited with clam for cod, while the lower hook, size 1/0 or 2/0, can be baited with a green crab or fiddler crab for blackfish or tautog.

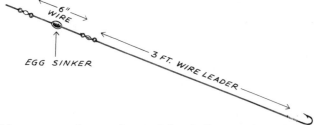

This grouper rig can be used in shallow and moderate depths. First attach a barrel swivel to the end of the line, then a short length of stainless-steel wire (about six or seven inches). Slide an egg sinker on the wire and attach another barrel swivel to the end of the wire. To complete the rig, tie on a three-foot wire leader and the hook.

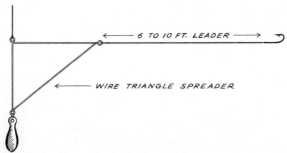

For fishing for red snappers and grouper in deep water this rig, utilizing a triangular spreader made from heavy wire, is a favorite. The rig has three eyes, one to each point of the triangle. One eye holds the sinker tied up close. The eye extending out holds the leader and hook. (Because red snappers and even grouper may shy away from this hardware, you should use a six- to ten-foot leader.) Tie your fishing line to the remaining eye.

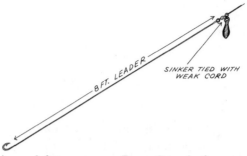

This rig is used for tarpon at Boca Grande from a drifting boat. A barrel swivel is tied on the end of the line and then an eight-foot wire leader is tied to the barrel swivel. On the end of the wire leader a No. 6/0 Sobey hook is attached. Then an eight- or ten-ounce sinker is tied to the barrel swivel with weak cord or soft wire. The hook can be baited with a small live blue crab, a pinfish, mullet or other baitfish. When a tarpon gets hooked and leaps or runs, the sinker will break off and you can fight the fish without the weight.

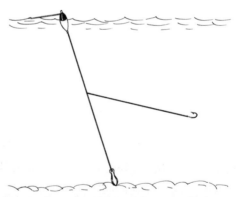

This is a shallow-water rig with a sinker on the bottom and a float on the surface of the water, with the hook suspended at about the middle. The bait is presented naturally while held in one spot in a strong tide (a float alone would drift away, taking the bait with it). And of course the float will indicate a fish's nibble or bite.

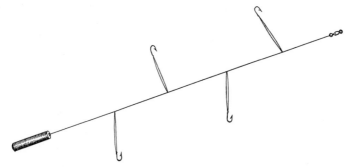

Here's a rig that is used in deep reef fishing off the Pacific coast for rockfish and lingcod. A heavy one- to three-pound weight or sinker is needed on the end of the line. Then up to four or five loops about eight inches long are tied at equal intervals. A ball-bearing swivel is placed on the upper end of the rig. A few inches of weaker line can attach the weight to the rig in case it gets hung up and must be broken off. The 6/0 to 8/0 hooks on the rig are baited with live or dead anchovies.

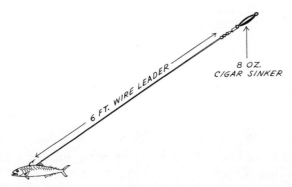

You can use this rig for black sea bass along the Pacific coast. Attach an eight-ounce cigar-shaped sinker to the end of your strong 80-pound-test line. Then tie a six-foot cable-wire leader to this weight, putting a No. 8/0 or 9/0 tuna hook on the end of the leader. The hook is baited with a whole mackerel hooked through the back and is lowered to the bottom.

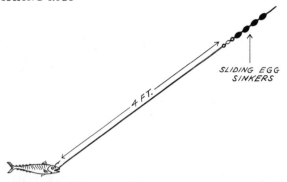

A somewhat similar rig is this one used for yellowtail in Mexican waters. Here you thread anywhere from two to six sliding sinkers on your line and then attach a barrel swivel at the end of the line, tying to it a four-foot leader and an 8/0 or 9/0 hook. For bait you hook a live mackerel through the lips and send it down to the bottom.

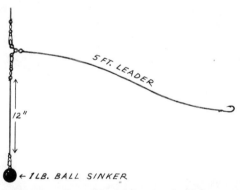

This rig is used to catch striped bass in the fast currents of San Francisco Bay Channel between the Golden Gate Bridge and Alcatraz Island. For bait you use an anchovy hooked through the lips or nose. The rig is mainly employed from a drifting boat and is tried at different depths, but for best results it should be close to the bottom. The one-pound sinker is required because of the strong currents near Alcatraz, but lighter weights are fine with this rig in waters where tides are weaker.

11. SURF-FISHING RIGS

This standard surf rig is the one most popular with surf anglers fishing from the beaches or from piers and jetties over sandy bottoms. For the smaller species, the leader can be short and the hook small; for bigger fish, such as striped bass, channel bass and bluefish, a longer leader and a larger hook can be substituted. Leader material is usually monofilament from 30- to 60-pound test, but it can be stainless-steel wire for bluefish. A pyramid sinker weighing from three to six ounces is used with this rig.

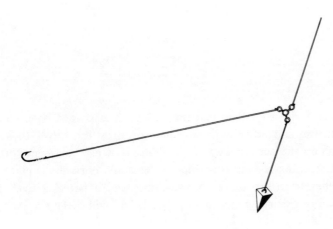

Instead of the standard surf rig above, you can use the "fish-finder" rig, so called because it makes use of the fish-finder ring and snap. The line runs through the ring and the snap holds the pyramid

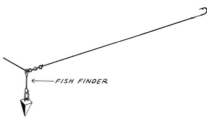

sinker, which is slipped on the line, with a barrel swivel tied to the end of the line to act as a stop. Then your leader and hook are tied to the other eye of the barrel swivel. It works on the same principle as the sliding sinker rig. The length of the leader and the size of the hook you choose depend on the species of fish being sought and your bait.

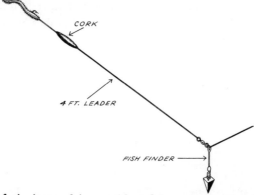

This surf rig is good in catching fish such as striped bass, weakfish, bluefish and other high swimmers. And it also serves to keep bait high off the bottom, away from crabs, blowfish, skates and other pests. Use an extra-long four-foot leader and a cork about eight or ten inches from the hook. A fish-finder and a barrel swivel can be added to this rig. Feeding some slack line will make the bait go even higher. The rig works best with any small, light, natural bait and is particularly effective with a single sandworm.

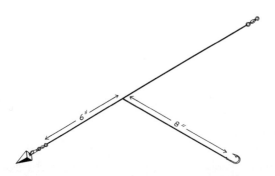

Surf anglers fishing for channel bass along some of the North Carolina beaches favor this rig. Using about two feet of mono, tie a barrel swivel on one end and a snap swivel on the other. Then attach a 7/0 or 8/0 hook on an eight-inch snell about six inches above the pyramid sinker.

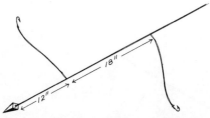

Along the Pacific coast, this surf rig is used for surf perch, croakers and other species. It has a lower hook on an 18-inch leader tied about a foot above the sinker and a second hook of the same length about 18 inches above the first. For sandy beaches and rough surf the sinker can be a pyramid, but for rocky areas you can use a round or bank type. Clams, mussels, pileworms, sardines and anchovies can be used for bait, depending on the species you are seeking.

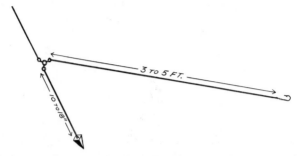

Another surf rig used along Pacific coast beaches makes use of a 10- to 18-inch dropper to hold the sinker and a long three- to five-foot leader to hold the hook. This permits the bait to float and move about freely and enables the angler to feel the nibbles and bites. It is used mainly for surf perch, croakers and corbina.

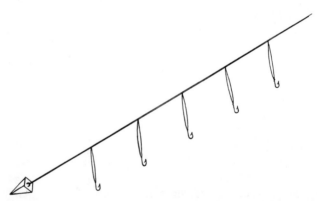

This pompano rig, adapted for fishing in the surf or from piers, consists of a long leader with anywhere from three to six gold-plated No. 1/0 hooks on short dropper loops spaced equal distances apart. Attach on the end a pyramid sinker three to six ounces in weight, depending on the surf and your tackle. The hooks can be baited with live sand fleas or bugs or pieces of shrimp.

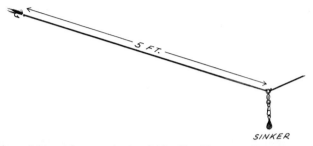

SINKER

When fishing for surf perch in Pacific waters you can make the fish hit a small fly with this rig. Attach a small snap swivel on the end of the line and add a small sinker to the snap. Then tie on a five-foot leader and put the fly on the end. This rig should be cast out and reeled in very slowly along the bottom.

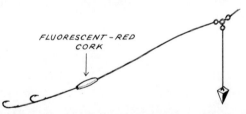

FLUORESCENT - RED CORK

One problem when fishing in the surf is casting so that the bait doesn't fly off the hook; further, the bait should lie neatly and naturally on the hook. The rig shown provides two hooks on the end of the leader to hold the bait better. Its fluorescent red cork keeps the bait off the bottom and attracts fish. This rig is especially effective with sandworms or bloodworms for striped bass, but it can also be used with clams, shrimp, strips of squid or fish or whole small baitfish for the stripers and many other species caught in the surf.

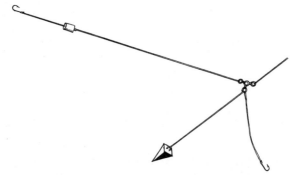

With this rig you can fish for many kinds of fish found in the surf at the same time. A three-foot leader and hook with a cork is attached to one eye of the three-way swivel. A shorter, smaller hook is connected to the other eye, to which the sinker is also tied on a short line. And of course the main fishing line is tied to the third eye. You can bait the upper or larger hook for striped bass, bluefish, weakfish and channel bass. The lower hook can be baited for northern and southern whiting or kingfish, croakers, spot, porgies, sheepshead, flounder or any other small fish running at the time.

12. SALTWATER TROLLING RIGS

This is the basic trolling rig used in salt water on all coasts for many inshore and some offshore species. You attach a bead chain trolling weight on the end of your line and then add a leader and the lure. The trolling weight will vary from two to eight ounces and the leader will range from a few feet up to thirty feet, depending on the fish you are seeking and the fishing being done. For most fish you can use monofilament leaders testing from 20 to 100 pounds, but for bluefish, king, Spanish and cero mackerel, barracuda and other fish with sharp teeth, wire leaders are better.

TROLLING WEIGHT

LURE

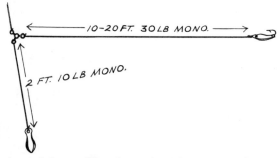

This rig is used for trolling for striped bass in the Chesapeake Bay area, where there are rocks, stone piles and other obstructions. It has a long ten- to twenty-foot monofilament leader testing thirty pounds, to which the lure is attached. A shorter two-foot mono leader testing ten pounds holds the sinker, which may be from four to twenty ounces, depending on the current. This light line will break if the sinker snags, saving the rest of the rig. A small spoon or other lure can be attached to the leader.

When trolling a surgical or plastic-tube lure for striped bass or bluefish near the bottom, it's a good idea to add a weighted keel up front even if you are using wire line. It helps prevent line twist, since tube lures turn and spin, and the weight will also hit every so often, letting you know when you are down near the bottom. The mono leader from the keel weight to the lure can be from eight to thirty feet long.

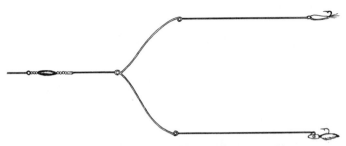

The rig shown above can be used to troll two lures on one line for the smaller game fish, such as striped bass, bluefish and mackerel. Tie a leader to each eye of a wire spreader. The upper leader can have a small spoon attached, while the lower one can have a jig. A trolling weight on the line just ahead of the spreader will keep the rig down while you troll.

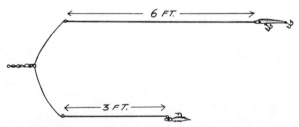

Another double trolling rig is this one used along the Pacific coast for striped bass. The wire spreader has a long six-foot leader on top, to which a spoon or underwater plug is attached. The shorter three-foot leader can hold a bucktail, feather or nylon jig. This rig can be trolled in shallow water without any added weight, but in deeper water a trolling weight in front of the spreader or wire line will get it down to the depth you want.

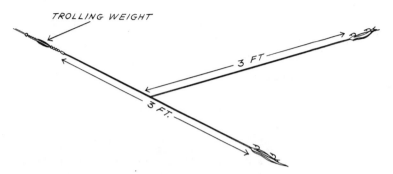

Still another double-hook rig is this one, used for fishing for summer flounders or fluke while trolling slowly or drifting. It utilizes a light trolling weight to which a three-foot leader and hook is attached. Then a second three-foot leader is tied to the middle of the first one. The hook can be baited with strips of squid and live killies, or dead spearing or strips of fluke belly.

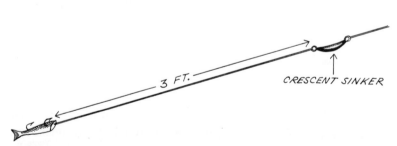

The Pacific salmon rig illustrated here is excellent in slow trolling or drifting for king or coho salmon. A whole or plug-cut herring is impaled on a two-hook rig and attached to a three-foot leader, which is tied to one eye of the crescent sinker. The weight of this sinker will vary from two to six ounces, depending on current and water depth. In working this rig, let it down to the bottom.

This is another rig for trolling for Pacific salmon. It consists of a four- or six-ounce trolling weight about two or three feet in front of a metal "dodger" or "flasher," and a herring bait on a two-hook rig another two or three feet behind the attractor.

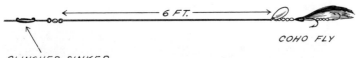

6 FT.

COHO FLY

CLINCHER SINKER

For trolling for coho salmon in shallow water near shore, try this spinner and coho fly combination. Tie a barrel swivel to the end of the line; add a clincher sinker in front of the swivel; then tie a six-foot mono leader to the barrel swivel, adding a silver spinner and a big two-hook coho fly.

WEAK LINE

A simple sinker-release rig for trolling or drifting can be made by putting an egg sinker on a light line between two barrel swivels. The two barrel swivels are also connected loosely by the stronger line of the leader. When a fish hits or gets hooked, the lighter line breaks, freeing the sinker, and you can fight your fish without the weight.

WHOLE
SQUID

HERRING

If giant tuna refuse to take a single trolled bait, it's a good idea
to try a gang of baits. Such a "daisy chain" can be made up of
several squid, herring, mackerel, or a combination of these. Usually
the end bait is a whole squid rigged with a single big hook. Above
it are teaser baits without hooks, rigged so they fall off when a
tuna grabs the end bait. They can also be plucked off the line by
a feeding tuna, holding its interest until it comes to the squid with
the hook.

A good rig to use when trolling for striped bass with a sandworm
is shown here. You make up a tandem-hook rig and run the first
hook into the worm's mouth and out about one-half inch below the
head. Then impale the second hook in the worm's tail. This worm rig
can also be used from a drifting boat.

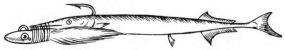

When snook are in deep water in the Florida Everglades country,
a good bait is a needlefish about ten inches long, with a three-ounce
yellow or white jig at its head. Run the hook of the jig through
the head of the needlefish and lash the bill to the body of the jig
with thread. This rig can be trolled deep in the holes and channels
and along the drop-offs where snook lie.

You can make up an offshore trolling rig using two or three Japanese feather lures by attaching a hook on a wire leader and sliding one feather lure down to it. Then, a few inches above this lure, attach a barrel swivel to the wire and add another wire leader above it. Now slip on another feather lure to rest against this swivel. Repeat this once more by adding another lure, and you're all set.

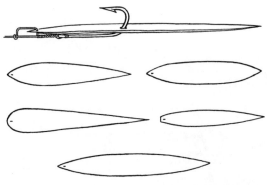

Strips cut from the sides and bellies of various fishes, such as bonito, albacore, dolphin and mackerel, can be used for offshore trolling. Most of the strips run from about eight to fourteen inches in length and taper to a point at each end. Some of the more popular shapes used for strip baits are shown above. The strips vary in thickness from about one-eighth to one-half inch at the center but are thinned or beveled along the edges. There are various ways of attaching these strips to a hook. One of them, shown here, makes use of a safety-pin catch that is formed from the stainless-steel wire used as a leader. This holds the strips in place so that it rides straight when trolled through the water. Strip baits are used for sailfish, marlin, dolphin, barracuda, albacore, wahoo and many other off-shore fish.

A quick, handy strip-bait rig can be made with two hooks, bending the barb down on one, then sliding the eye over it and bending the barb back to hold the trailing second hook. Then you impale a strip cut from a bonito, albacore, mackerel or mullet on the two hooks, as shown in the drawing. The rig can be used for inshore and offshore trolling for various species.

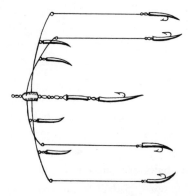

This "umbrella" rig, which was originally developed at Montauk, New York, is a multilure device making use of a wire spreader that holds several small plastic tube lures and is trolled deep on wire line. Some of the tube lures have hooks, while others are just hookless teasers. The idea is to imitate a small school of baitfish. It works best on bluefish, often hooking more than one at a time, but it also catches striped bass, pollock and a few other species.

13. OTHER SALTWATER RIGS

The live line or free line rigs, as they are called, are used for fishing near the surface or at medium depths for various saltwater game fish. Here, instead of using a heavy sinker, as in bottom fishing, you add little or no weight. The first rig shown above is merely a hook tied to the end of a leader. If your line is fairly heavy monofilament, you can tie the hook directly to it. To a light line, attach a leader of heavier monofilament. With a braided nylon or Dacron line, you can also add a monofilament or wire leader on the end and then tie on the hook. The barrel swivel is optional but is often used in a fast current where the bait may spin. The second rig is similar to the first, except that a float is added above the hook. The distance between hook and float will vary and should be changed to find the depth the fish are feeding at. The clincher sinker keeps the bait down in a fast current or tide. Both rigs are used with various natural baits, such as sea worms, clams, crabs, shrimp and baitfish. They are drifted as naturally as possible in the tide or current.

135

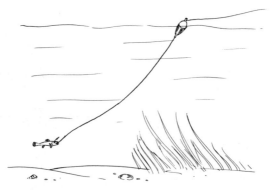

An offbeat method of fishing for summer flounders or fluke, which is often effective in shallow water, requires the use of a float high enough on the line so that the baits just clear the bottom or weeds. The hook is baited with a killie or spearing. The rig is fished from an anchored boat and the float and bait is drifted down with the tide.

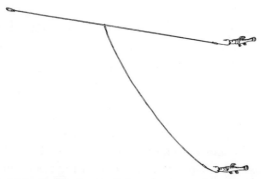

This special double-hook fluke rig is made by tying a 20-inch leader testing about 30 pounds on the end of the main fishing line. Then a second leader, of similar length, is tied at about the middle of the first leader. Use No. 4/0 light-wire Aberdeen hooks with this rig, baited with the largest killies you can get. With a conventional rod and reel, let out about 100 feet of line so that boat and rig will drift over shallow flats in water from three to eight feet deep.

The tandem rig here has a 12-inch leader tied to the hook of a jig, and on the end of the leader, a small silver or chrome spoon. The leader can be a light, coffee-colored stainless-steel wire for fish with sharp teeth, monofilament for leader-shy fish without sharp teeth. This rig can be trolled to locate such fish as Spanish and cero mackerel, bluefish and blue runners in southern waters. In northern waters it can be used for small stripers, bluefish, mackerel and pollock. But it is also effective in trolling or casting for many other saltwater species.

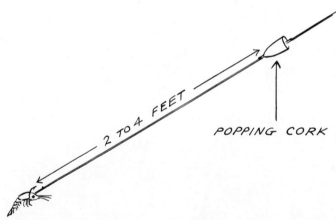

An effective rig for sea trout is made by adding a popping cork to your line and then attaching a small hook on a two- to three-foot leader below it. You can bait this hook with a live shrimp. Popping or jerking the rig every so often, so that the cork throws a splash, draws the sea trout to the scene, and they then see the shrimp and grab it.

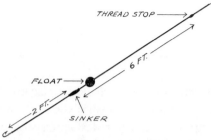

The rig above permits you to cast a bait with a bobber or float a good distance. A sinker is clamped about two feet above the hook and the float is added on the line above the weight. (This float should have a hole big enough to permit it to slide freely on the line.) Some thread or plastic tape is wrapped around the line about six feet above the sinker, to act as a secondary stop. The float drops down to the sinker when you cast, but in the water the sinker will pull the line through the float until it stops at the thread or tape.

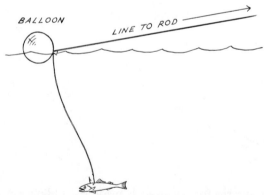

A good way to suspend a live baitfish just below the surface and drift it out in a tide or current or in a wind is by use of a balloon float. The balloon is inflated and tied with weak cord to the fishing line or leader, a few feet above the hook. You can fish with such a float from a pier, bridge or boat.

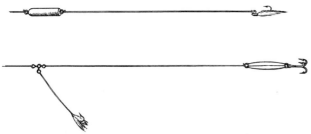

Two effective pollock rigs are shown above. The top one has a wooden dowel or float and a small bucktail. The wood float can be short and light for spinning rods and long and heavy for conventional surf rods. The nylon leader from the float to the small jig can be about 20 inches long. This rig is best for pollock in shallow water near shore. Striped bass will also hit it. The second rig is a diamond jig on the end of the line with a feather teaser about two feet above it. This rig is used in deep jigging or by lowering the jig to the bottom and reeling it back up. Besides pollock, cod, bluefish, sea bass, porgies and other fish will frequently hit it.

Anglers fishing for bonefish often use flies with a fly rod. But you can also cast a light fly for these fish with a spinning or bait-casting outfit with the rig shown here. You add a one-eighth- or one-fourth-ounce sliding egg sinker to your line and tie on a small black barrel swivel. Then you attach a 12-inch leader and a feather or bucktail bonefish fly on the end. The sinker provides casting weight and drags along the bottom when retrieved slowly in front of a bonefish, but the fly rides off the bottom, clearing most of the weeds.

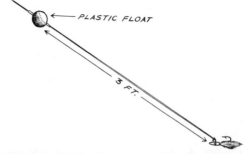

Seeking bonito in California waters, fishermen often use a fluorescent orange or red plastic float, and attach a jig three feet below a 20-pound-test mono leader. The rig is reeled and worked fairly fast so that the float splashes on top and attracts the bonito, which then usually hit the jig.

A somewhat similar idea is this combination rig for small striped bass in bays, sounds, rivers and surf. Tie a small popping plug on your line after removing the tail treble hook, then tie a 12- to 15-inch leader and a small jig on the end. This is cast and popped, attracting the stripers to the jig.

A good king mackerel lure is a nylon jig weighing about one and a half to two ounces. Add a second hook to this and then a mullet strip about three or six inches long over both hooks, as shown. Let this jig down to the bottom from a drifting boat, then reel it back with a lot of rod action. Other fish, such as amberjack, barracuda, jacks and even grouper, will hit this jig on many occasions.

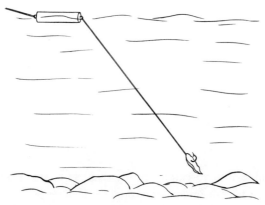

This rig is effective in shallow, rocky waters or over bottoms heavy with seaweed. It consists of a section of wood like a broomstick or dowel rod with an eye on each end. The fishing line is attached to one eye, the leader and a hook to the other—the leader just long enough to clear the bottom rocks or weeds. Almost any natural bait will do. The wood dowel both provides casting weight and acts as a float to keep the baited hook away from the bottom. It will also dip or move to indicate a bite.

Since it is impossible or at least very difficult to cast lures weighing a fraction of an ounce on the average saltwater spinning or casting outfit, a rig such as the one shown here is valuable to have in your kit. You merely take some nylon-covered wire, slip on an egg sinker and, making a loop, crimp a barrel swivel behind the sinker. Then crimp a sleeve or tube on the other side of the sinker to hold it in one spot. Finally, tie or crimp a snap on the other end of the wire, where the lure will go.

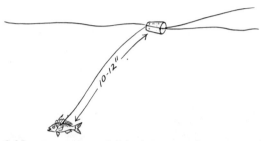

A dependable way to catch big sea trout is to use a live baitfish such as a small pigfish under a popping cork. The leader below the cork can be 10 or 12 inches. Popping the cork every so often will throw a splash and attract sea trout to the scene.

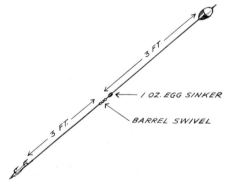

A good rig for pier or bridge fishing for Spanish mackerel or bluefish is made with a three-foot wire leader holding a double hook on the end. Tie a barrel swivel on the other end of the wire leader and a three-foot monofilament leader above that. Slip a one-ounce egg sinker on the mono leader and then a big float. The double hook can be baited with a strip of mullet or other fish, and the whole works drifted out in a tide or current.

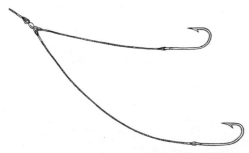

This two-hook rig for sharks holds a whole fish or a big chunk of fish as bait. It can be made quickly and easily by attaching a barrel swivel on the end of a long wire leader and two shorter wire leaders with big hooks to the eye of the barrel swivel. One of these leaders can be a few inches shorter than the other so you can hook the fish bait in two different spots.

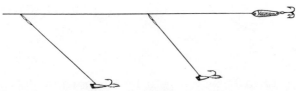

This rig is used to hook and boat hickory shad two and three at a time. It is made of two shad darts on droppers and a small quarter-ounce stainless-steel spoon-type lure on the end. Most effective when cast from a boat into schools of the hickory shad, this rig can also be used for mackerel, herring and small bluefish.

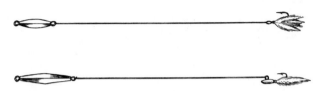

These combination lures can be used for many saltwater species. Remove the hook from a diamond jig and attach a nylon leader about two feet long. On the end of the leader you can tie either a feather teaser or a small jig. The diamond jigs provide casting weight and their bright flash is an added attraction.

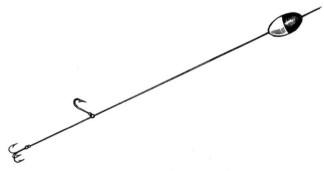

The rig illustrated here is popular for king mackerel fished from a pier. You use a large plastic float about five or six feet above the hook. A big 6/0 or 7/0 hook is attached to the wire leader, and a few inches below it, a treble hook. A live bluefish or other small fish is hooked with the big hook through the back, while the treble hook dangles free.

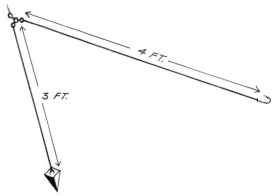

Fishing for snook from piers, bridges and boats, a pyramid sinker can be used, weighing from one to four ounces, depending on the strength of the tide. A four-foot leader holds the hook, while a three-foot dropper holds the sinker. You can bait the hook with a live pilchard, mullet, pinfish or shrimp.

FISH STRIP

This double jig and fish strip is often more effective than a single plain jig. Here a jig with the eye in the nose is slipped over the hook of the first jig. It should go on very tight, and you may have to bend the barb of the first hook to get it on. Then add a fish strip to the hook of the second jig. This combination can be used for king mackerel, barracuda, amberjack, snappers and grouper.

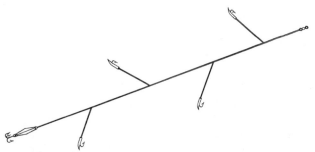

A cheap but effective mackerel rig can be made by taking a length of mono leader and tying a barrel swivel on one end and a snap on the other. In between you can tie four short droppers or loops, attach hooks and add tiny plastic tubing or feather hooks. The fishing line is tied to the barrel swivel, and a diamond jig can be attached to the snap on the end.

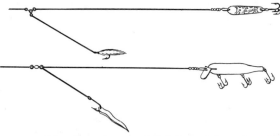

These two combination rigs are used by surf anglers fishing for striped bass. The first one has a three-way swivel tied about two feet above a Hopkins lure and a bucktail or feather hook tied on a short dropper. The other rig has a barrel swivel about two feet above a surface swimming plug and a short dropper with a hook. Pork rind is tied to this dropper about two feet in front of the plug. Both these rigs can be cast out and reeled to simulate a large fish chasing a smaller one. Stripers will hit either lure but usually go for the smaller ones on the droppers.

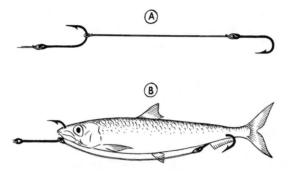

When fish are chopping off the tail part of a live or dead baitfish without getting hooked, try the two-hook rig shown here. A short length of nylon or wire with a second hook is attached to the first hook (A). The first hook is run through the fish's lips, while the second impales the tail, with the point facing down (B). With a live baitfish, the hooks can be small and of fine wire, in order not to kill the baitfish or to hamper its movements. This rig is often used on the Pacific coast for barracuda when these fish are striking short, but it is applicable to any saltwater game fish that has a habit of chopping off the tail of the baitfish.

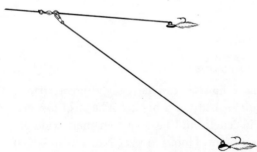

Although most anglers use one jig when fishing for saltwater game fish or bottom fish, there are occasions when a double jig will prove more effective. To a barrel swivel on the end of your line attach a short mono leader about eight or nine inches long and tie on a light jig. Then take a mono leader twice as long (16 to 18 inches) and tie a snap to one end and a heavier jig to the other end. Attach the snap to the lower eye of the barrel swivel. Such a double jig not only serves as an added attractor but provides two different types of jigs: one can be white and the other yellow, red or blue. And when you hook one fish, chances are good that another will grab the second jig and you'll be into a double-header. This is especially true of fish that feed in schools or tend to follow a hooked fish.

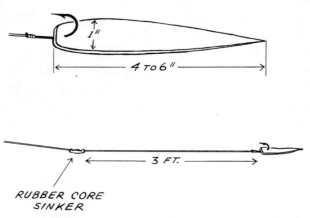

RUBBER CORE
SINKER

California yellowtail can be caught on a strip bait that is cut from the side or belly of a bonito. The strip can vary from four to six inches in length and be about an inch wide at the front end, tapering to a point. Hooks in sizes No. 1/0 to 4/0 are used to hold the strip, as shown. A lead-core sinker weighing about three-eighths ounce is added to the leader about three feet above the strip. Cast out the strip near a kelp bed or where yellowtail are present, let the rig sink a few feet, then reel it back with rod action to make it look alive.

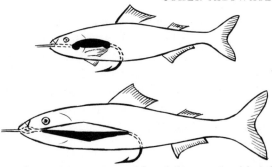

Here we have two ways to add weight to a dead baitfish and make it look more natural when cast or trolled. In the first method (top drawing) a clincher sinker is wrapped around the shank of the hook, which is then inserted through the mouth into the stomach of the baitfish, and the point and barb pushed out. To keep the hook in place, sew its eye into the closed jaws of the bait. The lower drawing shows how to add weight to a large baitfish. Cut a slit near the anal fin and insert into the belly a diamond jig attached to a wire leader. Pull the leader out through the mouth and sew it into the jaws. The size and weight of the diamond jig will depend on the size of the baitfish used. Here, too, you can sew up the slit and mouth.

Another way to add weight to a baitfish as well as an attractor is shown above. Add a hook to a large two- or three-ounce bucktail jig by bending the barb of the jig hook and slipping the eye of the second hook over it. Then impale a baitfish, such as a small menhaden, herring, sardine, mullet or balao, on the two hooks, as shown. With a soft-flesh fish such as the menhaden or herring, the second hook can be buried inside the bait. With tougher baitfish, such as mullet, leave the point and barb of the second hook exposed. This rig is very good in drifting in southern waters for king mackerel, amberjack, dolphin, barracuda, grouper and red snapper.

Use this rig to catch small fish for bait. Just tie a series of short loops on the light monofilament leader or line and add tiny No. 8, 10 or 12 gold-plated or silver hooks to each loop. Then attach a half-ounce sinker to the end. This rig can be jigged up and down from a pier, bridge or boat, and baitfish will often hit the bare hooks, though you can place tiny bits of clam, shrimp, worm or other bait on each hook.

Another good rig for catching small saltwater fish for bait is a series of tiny white or yellow jigs on short dropper loops, as shown. These can be trolled slowly inshore around buoys, in inlets, near bridges, piers, jetties and over shallow reefs to catch blue runners, goggle-eyes, pinfish and other small species.

14. USING
THE RIGS

You can tie the best rigs in the world, but you still won't catch many fish on them, or big ones, unless you also learn how to use them effectively for the various species found in fresh and salt water.

Take the simplest rig used in freshwater fishing—a hook tied on, bait added and then perhaps a float. If you are using such baits as worms, insects, frogs or minnows, choose the liveliest specimens you can find. They should move around in the water as actively as possible. If they stop moving or die, you can still interest some fish if you move the bait every so often with your rod or pole. Just an occasional twitch or a few short jerks will frequently do the trick. Or you can bring the bait in and cast or flip it out again. The sinking motion of the bait will attract fish to the scene.

If you are using one of the rigs with a float that slides up and down the line, cast this out to a good spot and let it stay there a few minutes, then reel in a few feet and allow it to remain there. Keep doing this until the rig is near the boat, then reel in and cast out again.

When using the freshwater bottom rig with a short snell with hook and sinker, you can cast it out to a good spot and let it sink to the bottom. Then put the rod in a forked stick on shore, engage the click on the reel and let the rod rest while the bait and sinker lie on the bottom. Every so often you can reel in a few feet and stop the rig in a new spot. In a river with a strong current, use a heavier sinker, casting it out and letting it lie in one spot, then raising the rod and permitting the rig to roll or drift downstream a few feet, to rest again. Repeat this until the rig is near shore, then reel in and cast out again.

When using the crappie or other panfish rigs with two hooks and sinker from a boat, lower them to the bottom and allow them to lie there awhile. Then raise the sinker off the bottom a couple of feet and lower it again. Repeat this at regular intervals so that the baits have more movement and attract more fish.

The catfish rigs in this book can be used during the daytime if the water in the river is rising or muddy or if the sky is overcast. But they will usually be more effective toward dusk and during the night. When you fish from shore, it's a good idea to employ two or three rods and cast the rigs out to varying distances to find out where the catfish are feeding. Then you can cast all the baits and rigs out the same distance.

In the case of freshwater trolling rigs, the simplest method is to use a fly rod and let out a streamer fly or lure, trolling these anywhere from 20 to 200 feet behind the boat. This is a very good way to take trout and landlocked salmon, especially during the spring of the year when they are on top and in shallow water near shore. Troll the flies and lures along shore and near the mouths of streams and rivers entering a lake.

Big brook trout and landlocked salmon will hit trolled streamers such as the Nine-Three, Supervisor and Gray Ghost soon after the ice is out. And instead of trolling just one fly, you can prepare a rig with two or three flies for these fish. Try trolling close to the boat in the wash, and if that doesn't work, let out more line. Follow the shoreline in a zigzag course, as this will often give the flies better action. You can also try raising and lowering your rod or grabbing the line and sawing it back and forth to make the fly dart forward and then drop back.

When using some of the rigs with buoyant balsa wood or plastic plugs that float, it is important to troll for both largemouth and smallmouth bass in the right spots and at the right depths. Troll for largemouth bass close to shore early in the morning and in the evening near weed beds, lily pads and hyacinths. And off the points and over submerged reefs. Troll in shallow water in the spring and fall, but look for the deeper structure when trolling during the summer months.

Trolling for smallmouth bass is most effective along rocky shores and ledges, over rocky bottoms, gravel and rock bars. In rivers, troll in the deeper pools and eddies. Use smaller spoons, spinners and plugs when trolling for the smallmouth than for largemouth bass.

It is highly important that the various walleye rigs in this book be lowered right on the bottom, and they should move at a slow speed for best results. In fact, back-trolling is often the most effective method, with your motor in reverse and the boat moving backward, the lines streaming out over the bow. Because the sinker or weight used with walleye rigs usually bounces on rocks or drags through weeds, it gets hung up pretty often. It should be tied to the rig with lighter line that breaks when the sinker gets snagged, saving the rest of the rig.

In using the muskie rig, try trolling it close to the boat fairly fast. Some fishing guides believe that muskies are attracted by the propeller and the wash of the boat, so they let out a couple of lines a short distance behind the boat. But there are times when muskies and pike are down deep. Then you should let out more line, add a heavier weight and troll deeper or even close to the bottom.

With the lake trout rigs you can troll in shallow water near shore during the spring and again in the late fall. But during the summer and early fall the lake trout are down deep. Then slow trolling with wire line near the bottom, in depths from 50 to 250 feet, is often required. Spoons, spinners, plugs and small fish such as smelt and sawbellies can be used. With a spoon, it's a good idea to raise the rod briskly and then lower it, letting the spoon settle back to the bottom. The important thing is always to keep the lure or bait close to the bottom. This means you will have to keep adjusting the length of the line, reeling in at times or letting it out, as the bottom contour demands.

Look for coho salmon in fresh water in the spring and early summer where alewives and smelt are plentiful. This usually means trolling in the upper 40 or 50 feet. Later the fish go into deeper water, and then you have to troll with cannonball sinkers, downriggers or wire lines to get down to depths from 50 to 150 feet. You can troll several lines at different depths until fish are caught. Then you can adjust all the lines to the same depth.

When using the various white shad and hickory shad rigs in this book you have to troll where the fish are concentrated—usually in the deeper pools, below falls, dams and rapids. This is where the shad congregate and rest before resuming their journey upstream. And the jigs, shad darts and spoons on these rigs should be trolled slowly down deep but can be given additional action by working the rod up and down at regular intervals.

No matter which freshwater trolling rig you use, you have to troll at the correct speeds and depths. If you see fish breaking or feeding on top or minnows or baitfish skipping, you can troll fairly fast to keep the lure traveling just below the surface. But most trolling will be done near the bottom over weeds, rocks, sunken trees, old creek beds and channels. The electronic fish-finders and depthsounders can locate such spots and even schools of fish above the bottom and are a big aid in trolling the most productive spots.

But you will have to experiment with boat speeds and depths until you find the fish's preferences. Of course, the type of lure you have will govern the speed of your boat. Most spinners, spoons and plugs work best at slow or medium speeds. Other metal lures, jigs, streamer flies and certain plugs perform better at faster speeds. Varying your speed will often bring more strikes than trolling at a steady speed. You have to keep changing speeds and working your throttle, depending on the waves, current, wind and the depth you are fishing. Your motor should be tuned to move at the slowest speed necessary without conking out. If your outboard is too big, you may have to bring along a smaller motor or an electric motor to troll at very slow speeds.

Steelhead rigs have to be drifted with the current so that the bait moves naturally as close to the bottom as possible without hanging up. Watch the tip of your rod and try to feel the sinker bouncing. If the rod tip stops nodding, or you feel the line tighten or catch, or the bait stops moving, set the hook. When the rig swings downstream toward shore, reel in and make another cast. In a fast river current you may have to cast upstream and use a heavier sinker to get down to the bottom.

The rigs that call for a plastic bubble or float work best with wet flies and nymphs. Here you use a light four-pound-test line with a light spinning outfit and cast the rig out into the current. Then you reel in slowly and retrieve the flies with occasional rod action to make them look like natural insects.

The rigs that have a popping plug or float in front of a panfish bug, jig or bait should be cast out and allowed to lie still for a minute or so. Then you pop the plug or float lightly and let it lie still again for a few seconds. Repeat—popping it, reeling in the slack line and letting it lie still once more—until the rig is near the shore or boat.

Some rigs can be used from a drifting boat that moves slowly in the current or with the wind. Here you can lower the plain bait rigs over the side of the boat and let out line as the baited hook passes over the best spots. You can also use one of the rigs with a float or bobber, and casting it ahead of a drifting boat. Then as you move toward the float, reel in the slack line slowly. When you reach the float, bring it in and cast out again. Or you can just let the float drift behind the moving boat.

You can also drift with some of the bottom rigs and trolling rigs used for bass, walleyes, panfish and even catfish. Here you let the rig down to the bottom, the sinker dragging as the boat moves slowly in the current or with the wind. You try to feel the bottom with your sinker and raise the rod when you feel it hit a rock or boulder or other obstruction. But if you drift over a hole or drop-off you lower the rod and even let out some line so that the sinker hits bottom again. Keep doing this, and if you feel a fish grab the bait, let out some slack line so that the rig lies on the bottom quietly and the fish can swallow the bait. Then reel in the slack and set the hook.

Some of the freshwater rigs are suitable in jigging for various species. For black bass you can use plastic grub tails, jigs, spoons and other metal lures. Anchor or drift over a good spot and lower the lure to the bottom, then reel in a few turns and start working it up and down. The same thing can be done for lake trout and coho salmon in deep water. Here you need larger, heavier spoons, jigs and metal lures; let them sink to the bottom, then either work them just off the bottom or reel them back slowly toward the surface with plenty of rod action. Pike will also hit a spoon that is jigged up and down, especially on humps or rises surrounded by deep water; they will usually grab it as it is sinking or fluttering down.

Saltwater-bottom fishermen are fortunate in having so many spots and locations where they can practice their sport. They can fish with their saltwater rigs from charter boats, party boats or drift boats, private boats, rowboats and skiffs, off shore, piers, docks, bulkheads, bridges and jetties. Some anglers look down on bottom fishing as being too easy, but there is much more to it than just dangling or casting a line and rig overboard and then waiting for a bite.

Most bottom fishing is best where there is plenty of cover and food for the fish. Since bottom fish of all kinds tend to gather in areas rich in such food as clams, oysters, mussels, crabs, seaworms, shrimps and small fish, fishermen seek out rocky bottoms, shellfish beds, kelp, seaweed and so-called offshore banks. In southern waters coral reefs are favorite hangouts for various kinds of bottom fish. And if you can locate a sunken ship or wreck you have a choice fishing spot. In recent years many artificial reefs have been created, and these also provide good bottom fishing.

Most bottom fish depend on the tides and currents to bring them food, and you'll find that fishing is usually best when the tide is running. Too fast a tide may make it difficult to hold bottom when the rig is lying still, but it should move a few feet when the rod is lifted. Most of the time you can lower your rig to the bottom directly below you. But when the current is strong or when you are fishing from an anchored boat, pier, bridge or jetty, it pays to cast the rig out, placing the bait in a better spot. And instead of just letting the rig and bait lie on the bottom in one spot, wait a few minutes, then reel it in a few feet, let it lie, reel in, repeating until the rig is under you. Then cast out to a new spot and begin again. This way not only will the bait have movement, but you will cover more spots, so that more fish will see your offering.

When your bait is directly under you, you can give it some movement—attracting more fish to the scene—by lifting and lowering it at regular intervals. By letting the sinker drop back and bounce bottom you will also know that you are down deep enough.

When fishing from a crowded party boat try to get to the stern, especially if you are fishing at anchor. The fish usually move against the current or tide and will come up on the baited hooks at the stern first. Another way to get away from the competition of the other lines is to cast or flip your rig a good distance away from the boat. Naturally you won't cast overhead if the boat is crowded, but you can flip your rig and bait out a good distance underhand without endangering anyone.

The size of the bait you use is important and how you hook it also plays a part in how many fish you will catch on bottom rigs. For most fish, a small or medium-sized bait is best so that they can get it in their mouths quickly and swallow it. With such baits you won't miss many fish. And it's a good idea to hook the bait so that the point and barb of the hook protrudes. Don't worry about the fish seeing the baited hook—most bottom fish pay little attention to the hook and grab without hesitation.

If you are after bigger game, however, you can use larger baits, not only because such baits attract the fish you want, but also because they withstand the nibbles and assaults of the smaller bait-stealing fish and crabs.

Knowing when to set the hook is very important in fishing for most bottom species. Most expert bottom fishermen develop a delicate sense of feel that enables them to hook a fish at the right moment. Too many anglers tend to be impatient and try to set the hook as soon as they feel the first nibble. Chances are that these are the bait-stealers. Usually it pays to wait until you feel a solid tug or pull, then raise the rod tip quickly to set the hook. With some species it is advisable to lower your rod and give some slack line when you feel the first nibbles. This affords them a better chance to swallow the bait and doesn't arouse their suspicions as much as a tight line and bait being pulled away from them.

With flounder rigs, use the lightest sinkers that will hold bottom. Some days and during certain seasons flounders want a bait lying on the bottom without moving. Other days, lifting the bait a few inches off the bottom and lowering it will attract them. There are anglers who like to paint their sinkers white, yellow, orange or red, believing these colors will draw the flatfish to the scene. But most anglers resort to chumming with crushed mussels, clams, cat or dog food or even canned corn kernels to draw flounder under the boat.

When using the various bottom rigs you should always be changing sinkers to match the tides, currents, wind and waves and the depth of the water. A sinker may hold bottom when the tide is weak, but it may not when the tide increases or starts running strong. Change then to a heavier weight. Likewise, if the tide is strong when you start fishing and you need a heavy sinker, this doesn't mean you should use that weight all day long. When the tide slows down or weakens, change to a lighter sinker. So it pays to carry sinkers in different weights.

With the surf-fishing rigs, one of the best techniques is to cast out and let your bait rest on the bottom a few minutes, then successively reel in a few feet and let it rest again until the rig and bait is almost up on the beach. Then make another cast and repeat the procedure. This reeling gives the bait more movement and covers more territory than letting the bait lie in one spot. Of course, if there's a rough surf, the wave action will work for you and all you have to do is reel in the slack line.

When fishing with a surf rig for channel bass you can also make the bait move and cover more territory. This can be done in a slough or trough where there is a strong current running parallel to the beach. Cast the rig out at the upper end of the slough and then slowly keep pace with the bait rig as the current sweeps it down along the bottom toward the lower end.

A fish-finder surf rig, with a cork and a small bait or a live bait such as an eel or a baitfish, can be cast out. Then slack line can be fed so that the bait rises or swims higher off the bottom. This keeps it away from crabs and small fish and also gives the bait some movement that attracts fish.

Surf anglers fishing with the pompano rig use a special technique that they believe enables their prey to find the bait more easily. They cast their rig, baited with sand fleas, at an angle and then reel it in slowly along the bottom. Then they walk a short distance down the beach and cast in the opposite direction so that the rig crosses the first cast. Reeling in slowly again, they drag the rig and fleas along the bottom, forming an "X." Finally, they cast once more so that the rig and bait sink to the bottom at the cross-point of the "X."

To use the inshore trolling rigs effectively you have to know your waters. Most inshore trolling is best over rocks and reefs, clam, mussel and oyster beds, near breakwaters, jetties, beaches, bridges, rocky shores and inlets and river mouths. And you should troll in tidal rips, strong currents and turbulent water. Look for birds diving or working, fish breaking or bait leaping, and troll there. If you see other boats trolling and catching fish you can join them, but do not get too close or interfere with their lines, which can be quite a distance out.

How much line you let out, how deep you troll, and how fast or slow you troll in inshore waters will depend on many factors. You have to take into consideration the tides and currents, waves and wind, the depth of the water, the lure or bait being used and the fish you are seeking. When the fish are feeding on top or close to the surface, you can troll faster with a short line and with your lure traveling just below the surface. And you don't need too much weight on the line. But when you are trolling deeper, especially close to the bottom, you slow down, troll a longer line—even a wire line— and use a heavier trolling weight. And you can bump bottom every so often with the trolling weight to make sure you are deep enough. However, you will have to reel in some line when traveling over shallow spots, rocks or boulders, wrecks and other elevations, and let out line when you reach drop-offs, holes and channels.

With any of the striped bass or bluefish rigs, troll faster and closer to the surface when you see these fish feeding on top and when trolling at dawn or dusk. During the daytime troll deeper, near the bottom. Deep, slow trolling for the stripers and blues is usually best at night too.

The lures you use will also govern the speed of the boat. The best speed is the one that brings out the best action of the lure and gets the most strikes. Here it's a good idea to release a few feet of line and test the action of your lure before you let your line out all the way. Some lures, such as jigs and eelskins and rigged eel or plastic eels, will bring more strikes if you give them a bit of rod action at regular intervals. Jigs, especially, should be worked in a short, quick, snappy movement of the rod when being trolled for striped bass and bluefish.

Pacific coast anglers like to troll with the spreader rig described in this book. Here two different lures, usually a spoon or plug on the longer, upper leader and a jig on the shorter, lower leader, are used. This rig can be trolled without any weight in shallow water, but in deeper water a trolling weight should be added in front of the spreader.

Along the Atlantic coast anglers favor another multiple-lure rig, called the umbrella rig, when they troll for striped bass and blue-fish. This rig should be used on husky tackle because you may hook two or three fish at a time. Employ a wire line, with a long 30-foot monofilament leader between the wire and the rig. No more than two umbrella rigs should be trolled at the same time. You can troll a bit faster for bluefish than for striped bass with this rig. When you get the first strike or a fish on, wait awhile until you feel more fish hit before reeling in—that is, if you want to hook two or three fish at the same time. This is of course a strain on tackle and angler, so most anglers prefer to fight one fish at a time for the most sport.

With the rigs meant for Pacific salmon it is important to find the depth where the fish are present or feeding. Usually coho salmon will be closer to the surface than the king or Chinook salmon. In trolling the coho fly rig, look for these fish near shore around kelp beds, reefs and in tidal rips and river mouths. Watch out for herring, candlefish and other baitfish and for coho salmon feeding on them. Troll the streamer or bucktail flies anywhere from 20 to 100 feet behind the boat at a fairly fast speed. One trick you can try is to lift your rod every so often so that the fly darts forward and even skips on the surface for three or four feet.

But when you are using any of the other Pacific salmon rigs you troll deeper, 20 to 80 or 100 feet down and often close to the bottom, especially for the big king salmon. The rig with the metal "dodger" or flasher can be used with a herring bait or with a plug or spoon behind it. This dodger gives the herring and lures more action or movement, to draw strikes. In strong currents and tides and deep water you may even have to use wire lines and heavy weights such as the "cannonball," with a sinker-release device that frees it from the line when a salmon strikes or gets hooked.

The double-hook summer flounder or fluke rig should be trolled very slowly. Here you can use two different baits and move the rig on the bottom along drop-offs, edges of channels and holes, and in shallow water, tidal creeks, flats and inlets. When you get a bite, release some slack line and let the fish swallow the bait before you set the hook.

With any of the rigs meant for offshore trolling for the deep-water, blue-water game fish it is very important to give the baits or lures the right action. Usually you troll four lines—two "flat" lines directly from the stern of the boat anywhere from 20 to 80 feet back; the two others from "outriggers" 60 to 130 feet back. Weather and sea conditions will determine the distance that a bait or lure should be trolled behind the boat. When the seas are flat and calm and the water is clear you troll longer lines. When the sea is choppy or rough you can troll closer to the boat. And some fish are boat-shy, while others, such as school tuna, will come right up to the boat and hit lures close in. Usually the best speed is one that leaves a white wake and makes the baits move briskly on top of the water.

The baits should skip or swim naturally; they may leap or dig down below the surface once in a while. Of course, baits rigged for swimming should stay below the surface most of the time. But all baits should look like crippled or frightened baitfish trying to escape from larger fish. It is highly important to keep an eye on the skipping baits at all times and watch for billfish rising and following them.

Besides rigged natural baits, you can use artificial lures in trolling for offshore fish. It pays to carry a good assortment of artificial baits and lures on days when fish want them or when you can't obtain natural baits or run out of them. Plastic squids, imitations of balao, mullet, flying fish, mackerel, eels and other small fish are often effective for such offshore varieties as billfish. Lures like Knuckleheads and Konaheads trolled at fast speeds also raise and hook billfish.

Wood or plastic teasers of various kinds that resemble small fish or squid can be used to bring billfish to the surface and near the boat, where they may see and grab one of the baits or lures with a hook in it.

Of course, where you troll offshore is also important if you want your baits or lures to be seen and taken by fish. Look for the clean, clear blue water, the edges, drop-offs, underwater mountains or banks, humps or reefs, and the canyons. Troll along weedlines where there are color changes and where birds are working over baitfish. Areas where dolphin are plentiful are good spots to try for blue marlin. For sailfish, troll the inside of the Gulf Stream and along the edge of the continental shelf. Sailfish are more active when there is a light or medium chop on the water than during a flat calm. In fact, most billfish seem to feed more and strike baits or lures better when the water is choppy or even slightly rough.

When you are trolling for dolphin look for weedlines, patches of weeds, logs, crates and other floating objects. Troll close to these or stop the boat nearby and cast lures toward the dolphin hangouts.

Many of the rigs in this book can be used from a drifting boat, and this is one of the best ways to catch a wide variety of surface and bottom fish in salt water. In drifting you shut off your motor, let out line and move along with the tide or wind. Your baited rig can travel anywhere from just below the surface down to the bottom, depending on how much weight you have on the rig. Of course, you need a fairly brisk wind or strong tide to drift-fish effectively. Also, it works best over wide areas such as reefs, shellfish beds and rocky patches, or over "banks" where fish are plentiful but scattered.

Drift fishing is successful because you cover more territory and present the bait to new fish all the time. It also gives your bait some movement and prevents it from getting buried in rock crevices, weeds or mud. The moving bait tends to frighten away smaller fish, crabs and other pests but is very attractive to the bigger fish.

Drift fishing is done a lot from party boats for various species from top to bottom. Such boats are called "drift boats" in Florida because they rarely anchor, but keep moving over the fishing grounds. Here, using a bottom rig, you can let your line stream away from the side of the boat. But you can also try to get near the stern or bow, and here you fish the other side of the boat and let your line stream under it; a longer rod helps keep the line away from the hull.

Let your rig down, and when you feel it hit bottom reel in a few turns and then let it stay there while the boat moves over the rocks, coral, weeds and bottom. Every so often you can drop your rig and hit the bottom with the sinker to make sure you are still deep enough. If the sinker fails to hit bottom, let out more line. If you still do not reach bottom, chances are you need a heavier sinker or the tide or wind is too strong for proper drift fishing.

Anglers using the fluke or summer flounder rigs described in this book do a lot of drifting for these fish. Here it is important to drop back the bait when you feel a fluke grab it. If you are using a spinning reel, open your bail and let out a few feet of line. Then put it in gear, reel in the slack and set the hook. With a revolving-spool reel, put it in free spool and let some line reel off the reel. Wait a few seconds, then put the reel back in gear, reel in the slack line and set the hook.

Anglers also drift for striped bass, using sandworms for bait. This can be done with a plain rig and hook, letting the worm stream out 100 feet or so behind the boat in shallow water. Or you can use the striper rig described earlier, with a light sinker and long leader, letting it down to the bottom while you drift near bridges, in inlets, bays and along the beaches. Other anglers drift for the bigger stripers with live bunker, mackerel and herring.

Some rigs can also be used in drifting for the fish that feed near the surface and down to 30 or 40 feet, such as the bluefish along the Atlantic coast, where thousands of party and private boats chum with ground bunker and drift while letting out a hook baited with a butterfish slab. The same thing can be done for school tuna, with a small live mackerel the best bait.

And along the Pacific coast drifting is done for yellowtail, albacore and tuna from the "live bait" and private boats. A live anchovy or sardine is placed on a small, strong hook. Chumming is done with live baitfish, to hold the prey near the boat.

Pacific coast anglers also do a lot of drifting for salmon. They use the rig with a crescent sinker and two hooks on the end of the leader and put a whole or a plug-cut herring on each hook. The bait should have a wobble or a slow revolving spin in the water. After you let it out to the proper level or depth, raise and lower your rod at regular intervals to give the bait more action, especially if the ocean is flat and calm. In a choppy sea the up-and-down movement of the drifting boat will provide this action. You can also try releasing several feet of line, then pause, repeating this every so often. It gives your herring bait more action, at different depths.

Drifting is also effective with many of the rigs for the larger offshore fish, such as the giant tuna along the Atlantic coast, where chumming is done with ground bunker or cut herring and a whole live or dead herring, bunker, butterfish, mackerel or whiting is let out on a hook as the boat moves along. You can let out one line to go deep without a float, but the others can have cork or plastic or balloon floats to keep the baits suspended at certain levels. You may have to add a bit of weight to the leader above the hook and bait to keep it down at the proper level.

The same thing can be done for sailfish, using a live blue runner, pinfish, small snapper or grunt for bait under the Styrofoam float rig described in this book. Or you can let out the baitfish on a plain rig with a light sinker on the leader to keep it down in deep water while the boat moves along.

Finally, we have the various rigs that can be used in "jigging" for many species in northern and southern waters. In jigging you lower a jig or metal lure down to the bottom and then work it up and down just off the bottom. Or you start reeling it back toward the surface, working the rod up and down. Such lures as bucktail, feather and nylon jigs weighing from an ounce up to three or four ounces are used for most jigging. But you can also use metal lures such as diamond jigs, the Hopkins lure and heavy spoon for many fish. Almost any fishing outfit can be used for jigging, but best results are obtained with the lighter, shorter rods from six to eight feet long with short butts, fairly stiff tip sections and powerful butt sections. Lines testing from six to thirty pounds are employed for jigging, depending on the tackle used, the area being jigged and the fish being sought. Usually the lighter saltwater spinning rods, bait-casting or popping rods and conventional rods and reels are utilized for jigging. But prolonged jigging can be tiring, so the lighter outfits are favored by anglers who do a lot of jigging.

In northern waters jigging with heavy diamond jigs, Hopkins lures and other heavy metal lures is done for cod and pollock. Here lures weighing from three to sixteen ounces are used, depending on the depth of the water, the tides, the thickness of the line and the type of tackle. In shallow water with weak tides you can select the lighter jigs weighing only three to eight ounces. But in deeper waters and strong tides, with conventional rods and thirty-pound-test line, you may need jigs from eight to sixteen ounces in weight. For cod it is best to let your jig down until it hits bottom, then reel in a few turns and work their jig up and down at this level. For pollock you do the same thing, but then after jigging near the bottom a short time you start reeling and jigging at different levels on the way up to the surface. Usually the cod and pollock take the jig when you give it plenty of action with the rod, but there are times when a slow lift of the rod or the boat rising on a wave is enough to interest the fish and cause it to hit.

Another fish that responds well to jigging when it is down below the surface is the bluefish. And in the late fall of the year, when schools of stripers are deep, you can catch them by jigging. If the regular jigging methods do not work, try casting the jig out, letting it sink to the bottom, then reeling it back, jigging on the way in.

When using the mackerel rig described in the book, you first have to bring your fish up to the boat by chumming with ground bunker, herring or other fish. Then lower the jig below the boat and start jigging it up and down. If there's a big school of mackerel you will often get two or three at a time on the small tube lures.

In northern waters bottom species such as porgies, sea bass, fluke and whiting will also hit a jig if it is worked close to the bottom. Here the smaller jigs weighing from one to three ounces are best. And these should be used on light spinning outfits with six- or eight-pound-test lines.

Jigging works even better in southern waters, where there are more species that will go for the lures. You'll get such fish as king mackerel, amberjack, cero mackerel, barracuda, grouper, dolphin, bonito, yellowtail and snappers at varying depths. White or yellow bucktail jigs from one to three ounces with strips of Mylar added work best. Some anglers add a piece of shrimp, a strip of fish, a small whole fish or pork rind to the hook of the jig. Your best jigging will take place over wrecks, artificial reefs, coral reefs and rocky bottoms, where most fish congregate.

Even Pacific coast anglers are going in for jigging and are finding that such fish as lingcod, halibut, rockfish, barracuda, yellowtail, albacore and bonito will grab jigs at varying levels, from the bottom to the surface.

One of the big advantages of knowing how to tie all kinds of rigs is that if the fish aren't hitting on a certain one, you can make changes or even tie a new rig better suited for the fish you encounter or the fishing conditions you run into.

And when using any of the rigs in this book that call for natural baits, you'll catch more fish if you bring plenty of bait and even two or three different kinds. As soon as the bait dies or weakens or loses its color or flavor or scent, remove it from the hook and put on a live or fresh bait.

15. CARE OF RIGS
AND TERMINAL
TACKLE

The fresh- or saltwater angler who does a lot of fishing and ties many rigs must have the parts and terminal tackle needed for these rigs handy. And the finished rigs must be stored properly so that they can be found quickly during a fishing trip.

Tackle boxes and containers of various kinds are a big help in keeping the different items separated and available for instant use. You should also have containers or boxes for the snaps, swivels, spreaders, sinkers, weights, hooks, leader material and tools that are used for tying rigs.

Nowadays it is no problem to find a suitable tackle box. Containers for your lures, terminal tackle and accessories are made in various sizes, styles and materials, such as steel, aluminum, fiberglass, plastic and wood. And they come in different sizes for fly-fishing, spinning, bait-casting and saltwater gear and tackle.

If you do just one kind of fishing in fresh water you can probably manage with a single tackle box. A spinning tackle box, for example, will usually have cantilever trays that swing up and out, with compartments of various sizes.

But if you do fly fishing and spinning and bait casting and trolling, it's a good idea to get a tackle box for each, because the lures and many of the other items will vary in size.

For saltwater fishing, tackle boxes are of course much bigger, with bigger compartments, to hold the larger lures, reels, sinkers, rigs, hooks, snaps, swivels and other hardware. Tackle boxes for saltwater fishing should be made of plastic, fiberglass, wood or aluminum so that they don't corrode and will stand up through the years. If a tackle box is too big, you will have difficulty finding a place for it on a boat, especially a small boat; even a regular-sized tackle box gets in the way on most fishing boats. So many anglers prefer to leave their tackle box in the car or locker or at home, removing the items that will be needed on each fishing trip. Of course, on the bigger fishing boats there are usually storage compartments, drawers or lockers in the cabin where you can keep your equipment.

Shorebound anglers in both fresh and salt water naturally can't haul around a heavy, bulky fishing-tackle box, especially if they have to do a lot of walking to reach the fishing spot. These fishermen can purchase special fishing vests with many pockets for small plastic boxes filled with flies, lures, snaps, swivels, hooks and sinkers.

When fishing from shore you can also use a canvas shoulder bag to carry some of your lures, hooks, sinkers, snaps, swivels and rigs. Here again, the small transparent plastic boxes are ideal for keeping these items separated. Such shoulder bags come in various sizes, and for freshwater fishing the smaller, lighter ones will serve the purpose. But surf anglers who plan to spend many hours fishing from a beach, jetty or rocky shore with bait need the bigger shoulder bags or knapsacks, with more room for the larger surf gear, terminal tackle, rigs and maybe even a sandwich or two and a thermos of coffee.

At home, of course, where you have a lot more space for tackle in drawers, cabinets, chests and various boxes in your workshop, garage, shed, basement or attic, the big transparent plastic boxes with compartments are very handy for keeping the various items separated but available quickly when needed. There should be one large compartmented tackle box or big container for rig-making tools and parts: cutting pliers, flat-nosed pliers, needle-nosed pliers, crimping pliers, nail clipper, monofilament and wire leader material, hooks, sinkers, trolling weights, snaps, swivels, spreaders and other hardware. If you do one one or two kinds of fishing, all this terminal tackle can usually fit into one big tackle box or cabinet—a small cabinet with drawers and compartments such as those used by fly tyers is ideal for the purpose—and you'll have everything you need to make rigs. But if you do all kinds of fishing you will need a separate box for each type.

When it comes to storing and using flies, spinners, spoons, metal lures, jigs, plastic worms and other plastic lures, you can run into some problems because of rust and corrosion and even insects such as moths. All flies and other lures with feathers, hair or wool should be kept under cover in tight containers. A few mothballs or flakes will help too.

Each year before the fishing season begins examine all pieces with hair, feathers or wool and try to rehabilitate any materials that are rust-stained, dirty or sparse. You can try washing the bucktails and other hair lures in warm water containing soap or a bit of detergent. Feather lures can be held with pliers in front of a jet of steam from a boiling kettle. If these cleaning methods fail, the only thing you can do is cut off the old feathers or hair and replace them. If the hooks are badly rusted the whole lure can be replaced, though hooks attached with split rings or other changeable parts can be switched.

The painted parts of a jig can be renewed easily with a brush or spray can, in the same colors or new ones. The small bottles of model airplane dope or lacquer are ideal for such work. So are the small spray cans with different colors, which dry quickly after spraying. Here, of course, you must protect the feathers or hair or nylon by covering it with masking tape where it is wrapped close to the metal jig head.

Metal lures such as spinners, spoons, metal squids and diamond jigs will tarnish and corrode, especially when used in salt water. It's a good idea to wash such lures in fresh water and let them dry thoroughly before storing them in a tackle box or container. Metal squids made from block tin can be polished with steel wool and they will get back their shine and flash in a short time. Dull or tarnished metal lures of brass, copper, silver or chrome can be rubbed with a metal polish, jeweler's rouge or special polishing cloths to bring back their original bright finish. Lures that have unpainted lead parts will turn black on exposure to air or water. Spray them with various colors such as white, yellow, orange, red or green, which are more attractive to fish than the dull lead finish. Some anglers even spray or paint their sinkers in these bright colors because they feel they attract more fish.

Nowadays most plugs are made from various plastics, and they do not require as much care or maintenance as wood plugs, which crack, split, chip, peel and otherwise lose their original appearance. Deteriorated wood plugs can be repainted by touching up the bad spots with a brush and enamel or lacquer. Or you can spray the entire plug with one of the handy cans of spray paint bought in any paint or hardware store.

Plugs should also be inspected to see if the metal parts and fittings such as screw eyes, hook hangers, wire and hooks have corroded or rusted badly. This isn't too bad a problem with plugs used in fresh water but can be a big headache with those used in salt water. All badly rusted screw eyes, hook hangers and hooks should be replaced with new ones of the same size; otherwise you may change the balance of the plug, which will affect the balance and action of the lure.

Soft plastic lures imitating worms, eels, squid, small fish or insects should be kept away from heat. Some of these will melt and soften paint or other plastics, especially the transparent plastic boxes. Wrapping each plastic lure in tin foil helps. Keep them in metal or wood tackle boxes, though there are now special plastic boxes that are not affected by plastic lures.

When it comes to storing snaps, swivels, snap swivels, spreaders and other hardware, there is usually not much of a problem. They are small and can be kept in tackle boxes and small containers with compartments, or the small cabinets used by fly tyers. But after they are used, especially in salt water, they may corrode and not turn readily or the wire snap may weaken from the constant flexing and opening and closing. Then they should be replaced with new ones. Such snaps and swivels are inexpensive, especially if bought in large quantities. The ball-bearing type swivels, of course, are more expensive, but they stand up better and do not have to be replaced as often.

Sinkers and trolling weights do not require much care and can be kept in any appropriate tackle box or container. The big problem is to carry enough different sinkers and trolling weights for the fishing you plan to do without making a tackle box or container too heavy. Since sinkers and trolling weights are always getting hung up on the bottom and lost during a fishing trip, you have to have plenty of spares.

Storing hooks can also be a problem, whether in a tackle box on a fishing trip or in your home or workshop. The big transparent plastic boxes usually make the best containers, and the ones with a lot of small compartments allow you to segregate the hooks according to size and pattern. Several such boxes can hold most of the hooks you will use for fishing or tying rigs. But do not put used hooks in the same box as new ones, for any rust will spread. In humid climates or in homes and boats with dampness, even new hooks will rust in time. All badly rusted hooks should be replaced. Except for the big-game hooks, most hooks are relatively cheap and can be bought in   boxes of 100 at a few pennies each.

Storing lines and leaders also requires some time and effort, but many anglers neglect this maintenance. Most lines will be in better shape for the fishing season if they are removed from the reels and wound in line-dryers. Of course, if you have many lines and reels, this isn't practical since you'd have to own a dozen or more line-dryers. You can wind some of the lines on heavy cardboard or corrugated board on which you record the pound test of the line and which reel it goes on. However, most anglers leave monofilament or braided lines on their fishing reels and remove only their fly lines. No harm is done to most lines, but it's a good idea to wash your lines and reel in fresh water if they have been used in salt water. And monofilament line that has been stored for a long time should be stretched before being put on a reel. Merely let out a couple of hundred feet, attach the end of the line to some solid object and back off with your drag tight and your thumb or finger on the line to keep it from slipping off while you stretch it.

Monofilament lines tend to get stiff and brittle in time, especially if they have been exposed to the light and sun. All such lines should be kept out of the sun when not being used and also away from oil, grease, gasoline, insect repellents and various chemicals. Store them in containers in a dark, cool spot.

Monofilament lines and leaders should be examined during and after a fishing trip, for nicks, fraying, weak spots and coils and twists. Cut off the first few feet if you see weak sections, and if the line is badly coiled or twisted try to remove such twists or use a new line, changing spool or reel.

Wire lines and leaders should also be carefully examined for bends and kinks. If the kink isn't too sharp you can usually straighten it out, but a sharp kink should be cut out of the wire line and a splice made. A leader should be replaced.

Storing leaders can be troublesome if they are not properly coiled and put away where they can be located quickly. After they are coiled, you can put them in some big clasp envelopes or plastic envelopes. Label envelopes on the outside, indicating the strength, length and type of leader within.

The same thing can be done with the completed rigs for various kinds of bottom fishing, casting and trolling. Putting them in smaller envelopes, label each with the type of rig and the size of the hook and the fish it will be used for. But do not put any lures or sinkers on any of these rigs. You don't know what lure or sinker you will need until you reach the fishing spot and find out which fish are running and what the fishing conditions are.

When you go on a fishing trip take along only as many envelopes and rigs as you think you will need that day. Of course, if you are fishing over a rocky bottom where rigs often get lost, make sure to bring plenty of spares. But having them in the envelopes ready to go will save you a lot of fishing time. Just grab the enevlope, open it, put on the new rig and add the lure, sinker or weight. Tying a complete rig at the fishing scene takes time, and you have to bring all the terminal parts with you.

When making rigs out of multiple-hook rigs, with several hooks spaced a good distance apart on the leader, a good way to store and carry them at the ready is by winding the entire rig on heavy cardboard such as corrugated board cut from boxes. You can even bury the hook points and barbs in the cardboard so that they won't stick or tangle.

The best place to tie fishing rigs and make leaders is at home or in your workshop. This can be done during the winter months or between fishing trips. Then the rigs and leaders will be tied properly with no hurrying or pressure, and they can be stored in envelopes until needed.

INDEX